T0283391

THE
LITTLE
HISTORY
OF
GLASGOW

THE
LITTLE
HISTORY
OF
GLASGOW

NEIL
ROBERTSON

For Kirsty

First published 2024

The History Press
97 St George's Place, Cheltenham,
Gloucestershire, GL50 3QB
www.thehistorypress.co.uk

British Library Cataloguing in Publication Data.
A catalogue record for this book is available from the British Library.

ISBN 978 1 80399 502 1

Typesetting and origination by The History Press
Printed and bound in Great Britain by TJ Books Limited, Padstow, Cornwall.

MIX
Paper from
responsible sources
FSC® C013056

Trees for LYfe

CONTENTS

INTRODUCTION

I belong to Glasgow, dear old Glasgow town. But something's the matter with Glasgow, for it's going round and round. I'm only a common old working chap as anyone here can see. But when I get a couple of drinks on a Saturday, Glasgow belongs to me.

'I Belong to Glasgow', a song by Will Fyffe

It's one of the best-known reflections – and certainly the most immortal – about the city of Glasgow. One that manages to capture so much of what we as locals hold dear about the place. Personally, it takes me back to weary walks home at ungodly hours after bar shifts in the city centre, with the raucous night still pounding in my head, and to chance chatty encounters with midnight drifters only too eager to set the world to rights and make my stroll pass all the quicker.

For Glaswegians are talkers, blaggers and storytellers. They love to wind each other up and to trigger a debate. They are friendly, no question, but it's more than just friendliness behind that desire for a good blether. Throw in some nosiness, eternal empathy and no shortage of opinions begging to be unleashed. Because Glasgow has a big heart, and with it a moral compass. Socialism runs deep in its waters and fairness is at the heart of the city's personality.

This book is most certainly not a deep dive into every facet of Glasgow's past. There are a million and one stories, myths and tangents that I could have delved into but what it is intended to be is more of a comprehensive summary. I've tried to cover all the big things while not delving exhaustively into anything, or anyone, in particular. Hopefully, I've achieved balance.

I've structured the book as logically as I can, with the first several chapters offering a chronological navigation through Glasgow's journey. Chapter 1 deals with the ancient history, going back to the pre-existence of the city and the early days as it found its feet as a fledgling settlement. It took a long time to establish itself and only became a pin on anyone's map long after Edinburgh, Perth and Stirling were well established. Chapters 2–4 cover a century each from 1700 onwards as the city became itself. Having set the scene and provided some momentum, I then break the remainder of the book into a closer study of some of Glasgow's pillars. This includes its people, the evolution of transport and education, our all-important sources of entertainment and the tricky subjects of politics and religion. You'll find it has had a passionate relationship with all.

There comes the question of what actually is Glasgow, geographically that is. I've stuck as much as is possible to the City of Glasgow, although notable mentions of the sprawling areas of Greater Glasgow do appear. That includes the highly populous surrounding regions of Dunbartonshire, Renfrewshire, Lanarkshire and others. Neighbouring towns including the Clydebanks, Dumbartons and Paisleys will come up, albeit minimally.

It's been a great privilege to put my city into words, to try to capture what truly makes it tick. As the chef, author and travel documentarian Anthony Bourdain once remarked, 'Glasgow is maybe the most bullshit-free place on earth and an antidote to the rest of the world.' Harsh, but fair. Which is Glasgow through and through.

1

THE ORIGINS

THE ROMANS

The mighty Roman Empire that dominated the continent of Europe met its match in Scotland, a fact that has been celebrated with cheeky ear-to-ear smiles and swollen chests across these lands ever since. The gladiators, the chariots and the rigid discipline of one of the greatest military dynasties in history were, it transpired, no match for the realities of The North.

In AD 83 much of the Scottish Lowlands were, like the rest of Britain to the south, under Roman occupation. Only challenging terrain, climate and the stubborn resistance of the Caledonians had prevented further incursion and the complete conquering of the island. This from an Empire whose reach extended as far south as North Africa and had consumed vast swathes of Europe. Damaging conflicts and fruitless forays resulted in the Roman leadership taking a simple and pragmatic approach to the situation, much to the delight of Scottish egos forever after. Emperors Hadrian and his successor Antonius Pius chose the *Game of Thrones*-adopted attitude to the wild Highlands – erecting two giant walls to mark the northern limits of their Empire and, in effect, lock in the northerners and abandon them to their own devices. In AD 122, Hadrian's Wall sliced through what is now southern Scotland and northern England. Stretching the limits further, Antonine's Wall spanned over 30 miles of today's central Scotland between the rivers Clyde and Forth. Although manned for several decades, the latter was the first to be abandoned as the southern armies soon accepted that northern Britain was a march too far.

Precious little remains of the predominantly turf-built northern barrier, with only the outlines of defensive ditches

What remains of the Roman Bath House at Bearsden, part of the Antonine Wall.

and very sporadic stonework still in evidence for the super keen. Lanarkshire, Falkirk and the Lothians hold several barely there ruined fortifications that would have been outposts along the wall. Chief among the remaining relics around twenty-first-century Glasgow are the well-preserved Roman baths, found in the affluent suburb of Bearsden, 6 miles to the north-west of the city centre. Built to serve the garrison of a nearby fort, the bath-house culture made the journey north with the troops, serving as one of their few luxuries at the end of a hard shift. Furnaces created air heat that would rise through raised floors for a steam room effect, and permit temperatures around 40° centigrade. Very much a social venue, the fort here was probably home to around 100 soldiers. Relatively recent excavations of the fort's latrine revealed insights into their rather extravagant diet that included well-travelled olive oil, hazelnuts, coriander and even figs! The Romans abandoned the fort around AD 170, destroying the site in the process.

Today modern life has fitted around the bath house ruins, with flats, a main road and hotels overlooking the site. More impressive Roman relics are on display within Glasgow University. The Hunterian Museum's permanent exhibit, 'The Antonine Wall: Rome's Final Frontier', now boasts finely detailed sculptures and artefacts from the wall.

THE WARRING TRIBES

With the Roman Empire in full retreat by the late fourth century, the suddenly liberated peoples of fragmented Caledonia were

The impressive Dumbarton Castle sits to the west of the city.

faced with new challenges of identity, prosperity and security. Tribalism was the predictable outcome as the people fractured into geographical groups. The south-west, including today's Glasgow and its environs, saw the creation of the Britons as a tribe. With mighty Dumbarton Rock as its centre of power until the late ninth century, dominance of the adjacent and advantageous River Clyde was guaranteed. The Rock still stands to this day, a rugged 73m-high mound now decorated dramatically with its own castle, neighbouring football pitch and offering spectacular views over the western outskirts of Glasgow and north to Loch Lomond. There is no better place to appreciate the scale of the importance of the Clyde, the single biggest contributor to what Glasgow would become in its heyday.

But that's jumping the gun a little, because the Vikings first played a role in shaping the direction that Glasgow would ultimately take. The image of a fleet of longboats tearing up the Clyde, packed full of foaming-at-the-mouth warriors is a tantalising one, and they subjected Dumbarton Rock to an ultimately successful four-month siege in 870. This particular defeat forced the Britons into a relocation of their seat, upriver and east to Govan, and the re-forming of their kingdom into something new, Strathclyde. As they did across the British Isles, and the wider globe, the Scandinavian settlers brought with them terror, progressiveness, ambition and intelligence. Securing permanent culture-changing victories over many of Scotland's isles, their impact on the south-west mainland was less strong, although it was not until defeat at the Battle of Largs on the west coast in 1263 that their spectre over Scotland was cast back to the choppy seas.

Elsewhere across the nation during all this turbulence, the tribes of the north-west and the east, the Scots and the Picts, had been united by Kenneth MacAlpin in 848 to form a single kingdom. This marked the pivotal step in the ultimate unification of Scotland and the triggering of a long line of Scottish kings to come.

THE GREAT SAINTS OF GLASGOW

Mythical King Lot, ruler over much of what is now East Lothian, was one of many regional leaders who opportunely emerged in the aftermath of the Roman occupation. Whether he actually existed or not will forever be unclear but, in the interests of a good story let's imagine that he did. Because the legend has it that he was also the father of Thenew and grandfather of Kentigern, both of whom would go on to become Glasgow's patron saints. The story goes that Thenew fell pregnant out of wedlock – possibly as a result of rape – and was exiled by her seething father to Culross in Fife. It was here, on the banks of the Forth, that she birthed her son Kentigern, who would be sheltered and raised by local priests.

Young Kentigern would go on to raise a Christian ministry in an anonymous place to the west called Cathures, aside the Molendinar Burn. This fledgling little place would ultimately become Glasgow. He did this with the blessing of the King of Strathclyde, at a time when Christianity was very much on the rise. An arrival from Ireland, St Columba was the single most prominent contributor. Landing on the Inner Hebridean island of Iona in AD 563 from Ireland, his community-building works planted the seed for many others to follow. Kentigern would go on to acquire the status of bishop and the affectionate name of Mungo by the mid-sixth century. So began Glasgow's story as passers through would come upon this calm, peaceful haven aside a river teeming with leaping salmon.

Blossoming at the lowest crossing point of the River Clyde, the high footfall and strategically advantageous position inevitably led to it becoming a place of interest for traders; not to mention St Mungo's converts, whom he would baptise in the Molendinar. His enduring base was therefore further ripe for expansion and Strathclyde's centre point very slowly began the transition away from Govan to what became known as Glasgu, or 'Dear Green Place'. Passing on in 603,

St Mungo was buried within the current cathedral, the epicentre of old Glasgow. A much-improved Gothic version still stands today, as pretty much the only relic of medieval times (cue envious glances east to Edinburgh) and one of the most impressive historic buildings in the country. Now sited in a detached and serene spot slightly to the east of the city centre, it's a moody yet majestic look back at another time. Cared for by Historic Scotland and open for worship and visitors, it has also featured in numerous historically themed films and television shows in recent years.

Ask a Glaswegian to name the patron saint of their city and a sizeable percentage will identify St Mungo, his is a role well-known. Yet few will associate St Enoch with anything other than the current subway station and neighbouring shopping centre. Yet Enoch was in fact Thenew, Kentigern's mother, a former co-patron. Magnificent modern-day tributes to both exist within Glasgow's famed street art scene, with multiple touching murals depicting the humble, gentle and giving nature of mother and son. Which brings us to Glasgow's coat of arms, depicting four objects 'that never', which eagle-eyed visitors will see dotted about the city. The tree that never grew represents a legend that saw St Mungo reignite an extinguished fire using holly branches brought to flame solely through prayer. The bird that never flew was a robin brought back to life by St Mungo. The fish that never swam was one he cut open to retrieve a swallowed ring that symbolised a renewed love between the King and Queen of Strathclyde. The bell that never rang almost certainly did ring and is thought to represent the ringing of the city's church bells in order to 'Let Glasgow Flourish',

A version of Glasgow's coat of arms.

the city's motto and words thought to have been spoken by
St Mungo himself in one of his sermons.

THE GLASGOW FAIR AND EARLY PUBLIC GET-TOGETHERS

This hallmark of local culture reportedly began in 1190.
Bishop Jocelin obtained permission from King William,
the Lion, to hold the event, the first of its type in the area.
Originally held around the cathedral, it would have been an
opportunity to bring items of value to market for trade. This
would have centred mainly around farming and agriculture
in the early years but food and drink would have increasingly
lured a wider audience. The River Clyde also began its role as
a vital trade route as word got out, opening up wider domestic
and international markets. In later times, the Fair marked a
holiday for the locals and would traditionally see a stampede
to the coast and to the islands of Bute, Arran, Great Cumbrae
and others. Going on a wee holiday 'doon the watter' remains
an expression to sneak a smile from any Glaswegian.

It is likely that much of the bluster and excitement in town
would in time have found its way to Mercat Cross, historically
Glasgow's most famous, and located where the Saltmarket,
Trongate and Gallowgate converge at today's High Street. A
visible pillar that marked a place approved for legal public
trading, its earliest recorded existence was in 1590. The
Tolbooth would also, of course, have been the place where
local taxes were collected, and surrounding buildings would
at various times hold courts, jails and council offices. Public

Once the centre of trade, Mercat Cross on the High Street.

hangings were also carried out there until 1813. A modern replica of the cross can be found aside the Tolbooth Steeple.

WARS OF INDEPENDENCE

While Glasgow was growing slowly but surely over the centuries following St Mungo's passing and the end of the Viking era, Scotland's wider story was developing at pace. Surging forward through the historical timeline, the late thirteenth century brought arguably the most defining chapter of the nation's history. The death of King Alexander III in 1286, followed soon after by the death of his infant granddaughter the Maid of Norway, created a terrifying vacuum in Scotland's leadership. Competing noble families aggressively argued their cases, while King Edward of England watched on with interest. With furious disagreement preventing any sort of coming together among the most powerful families in Scotland, it fell to Edward to propose himself as a conciliatory overseer and de facto kingmaker over the Scottish throne. He put forward the uninspiring John Balliol and the new king was ambivalently welcomed in by the Scottish nobility as king in 1292. A solution that suited Edward down to the ground.

Years of tension followed as Edward's attempts to manipulate and control Scotland got stronger and stronger, resulting in the capture and removal of the beleaguered Balliol as king and Edward's blatant seizing of the throne for himself. The first War of Independence between Scotland and England began in 1296. The heroic figure of William Wallace was to sear himself into legend during this time, which for many may be down more to Mel Gibson's efforts in *Braveheart* than anything owing to fact. But a sensationalised Hollywood story aside, Wallace upset the hierarchy among the Scots' nobility and was elevated as the chosen one to lead a hugely outmatched army to victory at the Battle of Stirling Bridge in 1297, and even a subsequent daring invasion of northern England. Although factual knowledge of it is sketchy at best, the smaller-scale Battle of the Bell o' the Brae was supposedly fought in the area around Glasgow Cathedral and neighbouring 'Glasgow Castle' at the time that Wallace was rising to prominence. An occupying English garrison was attacked from both front and rear on, or very near, the village's

High Street and the outnumbered Scots were victorious, with Wallace personally slaying the English commander, Earl Percy. The castle may have been the home of prominent Wallace ally Bishop Wishart or that of a residing English bishop, but in any case, it ceased to exist many centuries ago. Had Glasgow seen its first battle?

A more stirring and odds-defying tale than Wallace's the nation has never seen, yet the high was short-lived. Wallace was betrayed and captured in 1305 at Robroyston in north-east Glasgow, with his last night in Scotland spent at Dumbarton Castle before the long journey to a brutal torture and execution in London. Of course, history and movie buffs will know that was far from the end of the matter and leading nobleman Robert Bruce stepped up as the new talisman to continue the war against England well into the fourteenth century. Appointed King of Scots, he recorded another improbable victory at Bannockburn near Stirling in 1314 and became a long-running thorn in the side of multiple English kings. In 1357 Scotland achieved its full independence.

Although recognised as a burgh in 1175, Glasgow was not a big player during any of this period. It didn't have a significant harbour or a military stronghold in the way that an Edinburgh or Stirling did, and was not set up for large-scale defence. On the topic of fearsome strongholds though, Glasgow and its surrounding areas did hold both Dumbarton Castle to the west and Bothwell Castle in South Lanarkshire, south-east of the city today. The latter is among the most historically intriguing of all in Scotland and was a staging point during and after the Bannockburn battle for the gathered English armies. It had also been besieged in 1301 by Edward's

armies, numbering around 7,000 men and a famous siege
engine named 'le berefrey'. It still took several weeks of them
knocking loudly on the door before the defenders succumbed.
Bothwell then went on to become the base for the dreaded
Aymer de Valence, Edward's Warden of Scotland.

THE LATER MIDDLE AGES AND MARY, QUEEN OF SCOTS

Without a central medieval historic ruin to Glasgow's name,
the closest remaining example is the poignantly atmospheric
Crookston Castle in Pollok to the south-west. Built around
1400 by Sir Alexander Stewart, the Earl of Lennox, it was
originally a three-storey keep. Involved in an uprising against
James IV, Lennox's castle fell under siege in 1489 and was
badly damaged by that and a further siege in 1544. It is
thought that Mary, Queen of Scots and Lord Darnley were
betrothed here, though it has been largely forgotten about
ever since. Surprisingly it remains in impressive condition,
with an intact tower and atmospheric interior rooms asking
to be explored. Meanwhile, the city was elevated from its
bishopric status to Archdiocese of Glasgow in 1492, with
Glasgow University having been founded in 1451 and a
blossoming status as a centre of religion and academia by
now unfolding. The university was the fourth oldest to be
established in the English-speaking world. First located within
the cathedral buildings, the centre of learning would move
to its own premises on the High Street and eventually west
to its current location dramatically overlooking Kelvingrove
Park in the 1600s. Glasgow High School dates back to the

The atmospheric ruins of Crookston Castle.

twelfth century and would have also been housed within the cathedral. Although records only began several hundred years later, Latin and grammar would have been central to the teachings.

The Reformation of the mid-1500s brought a wave of destruction to the hitherto unchallenged world of religion in these lands. The long-standing relationship with France (still referred to as the Auld Alliance) was eroded in place of a stronger one with England and the Stewart dynasty of ruling monarchs faced an existential crisis. Mary, Queen of Scots was at the heart of this latest unrest – a French-raised, Catholic ruler elevated to the Scottish throne at the tender age of a mere six days. Immediately placed in the centre of a power struggle between the French and King Henry VIII of England, she first came to Scotland to take the reins as a teenager and bravely attempted to bridge the growing Catholic–Protestant divide. Throw in multiple doomed marriages, several love-fuelled murders, political betrayal, imprisonment, defeat in battle and ultimately the long road south to Fotheringhay for execution in 1587 and the impossibility of her task becomes clear. So died possibly the most tragic character in Scotland's tapestry, no mean feat.

Mary did have further connections to Glasgow in that it is thought she penned the letter that doomed her in Provand's Lordship, the oldest surviving building in the city and another well worth a visit just across the road from the cathedral. Known as the Casket Letters, the words were for her lover the Earl of Bothwell, and were used as evidence against her and proof of intent to murder her previous husband, Lord Darnley, by Queen Elizabeth of England, who would ultimately go on to order Mary's execution. She also inspired several battles in the vicinity. The Battle of Glasgow of 1544 was fought during her early reign between the Earls of Lennox and Arran, with the latter routing the former and taking Glasgow and the castle in retribution for Lennox's perceived treachery for fancying the throne for himself. The castle defenders are said to have been conned into surrendering, then hanged for their loyalty to Lennox, who had already fled to his stronghold at Dumbarton. This savage act triggered another conflict between the Earl of Glencairn, a Lennox ally, and Arran's forces, with Arran again victorious, in what is known as the first Battle of the Butts. Occurring just to the east of the city centre, this crushed Lennox's designs for power and he fled to England and exile. At the other end of Mary's tenure, her ultimately decisive defeat at the Battle of Langside in 1568 was also fought what was then a few miles to the south of Glasgow, and she was captured shortly afterwards.

During all of this, Glasgow Cathedral was, curiously, one of the few centres of Catholicism not to be decimated as the Roman Church was aggressively replaced by Protestantism. John Knox was the most vocal critic, the outspoken Presbyterian preacher so bent on pushing through the Reformation and dooming Mary in particular. Today, a 12ft statue of Knox glares down at the cathedral that eluded his all-consuming tsunami from the neighbouring Necropolis graveyard. But, as with the Wars of Independence, Glasgow's as-yet fairly peripheral role in the Scottish power struggles perhaps sheltered it from the tumult occurring elsewhere across the nation. The thought that by far the most populous city in Scotland should be not much more than a bystander to such momentous events is certainly a hard one to grasp.

SEVENTEENTH CENTURY

But with each passing decade that role was changing and domestic economic activity very slowly started to drift west, migrating from the historic hubs on Scotland's east coast. Glasgow became a Royal Burgh in 1611, following on from the Union of the Crowns with England in 1603. This saw Mary, Queen of Scots' son James elevated to the thrones of both Scotland and England. Although it would be over a century before the nations were formally united, this was the first tentative step towards, ultimately, much closer ties between the two. But it was a tough century for the Scottish economy in the lead up to the formal union as relative geographic isolation from the European continent and blocked access to England's imperial markets in America left the country's export potential crippled. Even King James VI migrated his court to London and his reign saw him show little interest in, or affection towards, Scotland. If anything the Union of the Crowns had only weakened Scotland's position and standing in the world. Quite what James's mother would have made of that can only be imagined.

Meanwhile, Glasgow's population was growing, and its limits expanding. But a plague outbreak in 1645–46 – centred in the most crowded area around the High Street but also in nearby Paisley – and the Great Fire of 1652 were dramatic setbacks to the city's gathering progress. The inferno tore through and destroyed a third of the city over a torrid eighteen hours, leaving in excess of 1,000 families homeless. It too originated in the High Street, in the home of a James Hamilton, and spread quickly to his neighbours in Trongate and Saltmarket. Without a proper fire department to speak of, locals largely had to futilely fight the flames themselves, with the damage to the primarily wood-constructed buildings proving devastating. With domestic candles blamed as the cause, the city's candlemakers were exiled away from the burgh centre to the area that forever after took the name Candleriggs.

Today Scotland excels in exports including seafood, beer, gin, beef and, of course, whisky. Going further back, it excelled in the export of the fruits of heavy industry. Indeed Scotland, and Glasgow in particular, would go on to become a world leader in this area and it has always been a nation with much to offer the world through trade. But throughout the 1600s legislation in the form of the English Navigation Acts was designed to exclude non-English traders from operating in their new lucrative colonial markets and the economic cost of this exclusion took a heavy toll on their neighbour to the north. Many have speculated that this may have been a deliberate tactic.

Wider-reaching political goings on were also shaping this simmering hostility. King James VI's successor, King James VII of Scotland and II of England, was dethroned in 1688 as part of the latest move towards Protestantism across Britain. His Dutch son-in-law, William of Orange, invaded England with the backing of many within the English Parliament and took the throne of both nations in one of the most dramatic and brazen moments in British history. James, meanwhile, fled to France. So was born the term 'Jacobite', associated with those who supported James, the deposed Catholic monarch. The 1600s would close with a series of violent clashes across Britain and Ireland, with tensions on the issue still lingering to this day. Some within Glasgow's population have some particularly strong feelings on the matter, as is most evident through the organised and contentious Orange Order marches through the city and the sectarian divisions that emanate whenever Celtic and Rangers clash over a football. I'll be returning to this in later chapters of the book.

The growing economic crisis, though, came to a head with what became known as the Darien Scheme. Born out of a frustration that England was not keen to let Scotland play in its sandpit (legally at least), the Scottish Parliament was keen to break the monopoly of the East India Company over trade access to the West Indies, Africa and the Americas. In essence, the idea was to establish a springboard colony in Darien, Panama, and in 1698 a small army of colonists were sent across the Atlantic to begin Scotland's own mini-empire. Needless to say, it was an ignominious disaster as the climate, lack of resources and planning and, catastrophically, the arrival of most-displeased competing Spanish imperial forces, sent the colonists scarpering for home in embarrassment.

The economic road ahead for Scotland could only get brighter, and Glasgow would soon be called on to do the heavy lifting.

2

THE EIGHTEENTH CENTURY AND THE COMING OF THE INDUSTRIAL REVOLUTION

THE SCOTTISH ENLIGHTENMENT

Today it is from Scotland that we get rules of taste in all the arts, from epic poetry to gardening.

So said the great writer Voltaire in 1762, one of many qualified minds that was impressed with this new Scottish intellectual outlook. For the eighteenth century saw an explosion of talent come to the fore across the nation, with impacts and legacies that touched the whole world. Philosophers like David Hume and Adam Smith were joined by engineers and architectural titans of the time like James Watt and Robert Adam, medical pioneers such as William Cullen, literary giants including Sir Walter Scott and, of course, numerous poets, among them arguably Scotland's most famous son, Robert Burns. The latter's all-too-short life spanned the second half of the century and saw him pen some of the most immortal words ever written. To this day – and I know as I was very enthusiastically one of them – schoolchildren compete in recitals of his works from 'To a Haggis' to 'Tam o'Shanter' and statues, plaques and tributes to him are dotted around across the planet. Burns's home turf was the south-west of Scotland, Ayrshire and Dumfriesshire, but he is known to have visited Glasgow several times. His superbly maintained childhood home in the village of Alloway can be reached in under an hour's drive from the city.

With the new century began a new wave of academic and creative thinking. Scots were considering their place in this new world – a world that, to a large extent, they were at the centre of. Usually spoken in the same breath as how we stopped the Romans, Scots of today like to think we invented pretty much everything. Television, telephones, penicillin, football, the refrigerator, the flushing toilet … they'd have you believe that these and countless other life-changing inventions can all be traced back to little old Scotland. Astonishingly, they're not wrong. But, as with most things up to this point in time, Edinburgh gathered in the majority of the plaudits. The growing university did, however, start the noise around Glasgow's intellectual potential and would eventually have back-up in 1796 with the Andersonian Institute, which would go on to become the separate Strathclyde University.

In 1737 'The Father of Modern Economics', Adam Smith, enrolled at Glasgow University as a teenager. He would go on to create the foundations for free market economic theory, and received his professorship there in 1751. Droves of students from across Europe came to learn under him, with morality and empathy joining wider economic theory at the heart of his lectures. James Watt, who would become fundamental to the advancement of the steam engine among many other things, worked there as an instrument maker and repairer in the mid-1700s. By the 1770s, his engines were dramatically improving the efficiency of steam power and this would have a lasting impact on industry worldwide. Watt's friend and fellow lecturer Joseph Black was a pioneer in experimentation with oxygen, hydrogen and carbon dioxide and another of the university's great contributors. William Hunter became a world leader in chemistry and physics – his legacy being the Hunterian Museum that still resides within the university and was Scotland's first public museum in 1807, showcasing his personal collection of books, art, artefacts, medals and more. It was all go.

THE JACOBITES AND THE UNION

We have already touched on the Union of the Crowns, the rise of Protestantism and the downfall of the Stuart monarchs. What we haven't covered yet is the historic 1707 Treaty of Union, in effect the formation of the relationship that still endures between Scotland and England. Scotland joined with England and Wales to form the new kingdom of Great Britain. Unlike more recent processes regarding the Union, this decision was not one made by the people, by referendum, but by a handful of governing 'commissioners' who had become fed up with Scotland's enforced isolation from the lucrative markets of the Empire, not to mention the embarrassment of the Darien Scheme. While this pact presented great economic opportunity for the kingdoms involved, political and religious resentment continued to simmer in Scotland throughout these soon-to-be-enlightened times. Outrage at the permanency of a decision that affected so many being made by so few resulted in angry demonstrations across the nation, and I'll return to the delicate subject of the Union when we can delve deeper into the world of Scottish politics.

Surrounding these constitutional changes there had inevitably been conflict. James II of England and VII of Scotland had been sent off to France in exile in late 1688, but still held significant support – largely among those of a Catholic persuasion – amongst Britons who felt monarchs could not be removed and held a divine right to the throne based on their family line. His claim also had significant backing from across Europe, particularly France. In addition to the issue of Scottish independence and the Union, this separate anger spilled into the eighteenth century and culminated in large-scale battles at Sherrifmuir and Preston (1715) and, much later, Culloden (1745). The latter brought a savagely definitive conclusion to the Jacobite cause.

James III took on his father's claim after his passing in 1701, leading the ill-fated 1715 Jacobite campaign in Scotland and northern England. Prince Charles Edward Stuart, grandson of the originally exiled James, continued yet further with another major uprising in 1745. Rallying support from his primary base in the north of Scotland, his Jacobite forces certainly passed through Glasgow on their increasingly optimistic marches. A warm welcome is not thought to have been forthcoming, with the Lord Provost at the time, the no-nonsense Andrew Cochrane, refusing to fund or support the campaign from the city's coffers. In the end he had to give in, as the buoyant army would have been almost literally battering down his door, but it was a grudging bare minimum that was offered up (which Cochrane made sure to get back with interest from the British government after the campaign collapsed). For the 'Bonnie' Prince soon lost his promising early momentum and found his wearied and increasingly beleaguered army forced to engage at Culloden Moor just outside Inverness. The British forces under the Duke of Cumberland soundly defeated the shattered Jacobites in what remains the last major land battle fought on British soil. In the merciless aftermath, surviving Highlanders and prominent Jacobite supporters were stripped of their land, with many forced to leave Scotland altogether in what became known, infamously, as the Highland Clearances. Evicted from their land and homes by profit-seeking landowners, whole settlements were abandoned and replaced by large-scale sheep grazing, decisively depopulating the Highlands to a level that it has never recovered from.

This, combined with the Lowland Clearances stemming from changes in agricultural practices and land commercialisation, created an unprecedented movement of families seeking employment throughout much of the second half of the eighteenth century. Many made the bold choice (for some it was not optional) to try their luck in America and the British colonies, while others headed to swelling urban areas, including Glasgow. And this surge necessitated the beginnings of town planning in the 1770s, under the eye of surveyor James Barrie. A new grid system of streets stretched away from Ingram Street and westwards towards Blythswood Square. Garden boundary limits for residents and newly paved streets brought practicality and structure to what must previously have been a free-for-all. The sprinkling of villages around the High Street slowly merged into one and Glasgow became more and more appealing as a place to live and work. At this time, the mills and linen industry were the destiny of many.

LINEN

While Glasgow would go on to command a world lead in heavy industry production, it was linen that first sparked large-scale economic activity and possibility. At its peak the industry was an employer of tens of thousands of workers across the nation, and this at a time when Glasgow's own population was scarcely in five figures.

The sixteenth to the eighteenth centuries had seen some tentative industrial activity in fields including pottery, a soap works and paper manufacturing. The Delftfield Pottery was Glasgow's, and Scotland's, first large-scale manufacturer, being established in the 1740s and producing a wide range of products for local and international buyers. The 'soaperie' was an interesting case. Whale oil was among the key ingredients used in the manufacture, although grand plans for an associated Glasgow-based whaling fleet never came to fruition. The soaperie itself would go on to moderate success over several decades, despite not being a large-scale employer. It burned down in 1777, effectively killing the business... and presumably sending hygiene standards spiralling. John Smith & Son booksellers was another. Founded in 1751, it is probably the oldest independent bookseller in the world.

Largely a supplier of academic reading material for universities, it still exists within numerous university campuses. And we can't forget the pioneering chemical experiments of Charles Tennant and Charles Mackintosh in the 1790s, which would ultimately result in the creation of, among other things, the waterproof jacket, or 'mackintosh'.

These early rumblings were to be dwarfed by textiles, however, and the Industrial Revolution that changed the world. From around 1760, incomes and population numbers underwent sustained growth, with Britain established as the economic world leader. While financial equality had a very long way to go, standards of living across Britain began to rise as a result of an exciting wave of employment opportunities. To a large extent, the textile trade began as a work-from-home industry, often seeing women employed on a part-time basis to spin flax into yarn for factories. The laborious process would become highly mechanised but the early years saw only handweaving and no doubt plenty of furrowed brows and well-worn fingertips. The East End was particularly prominent in this work, though by the 1770s it was the main industrial activity of the city and Glasgow became Scotland's linen capital.

THE MILLS

The arrival of cotton on the scene around this time accelerated the economic growth. The century drew to a close with the opening of several dozen water-powered mills across the west of Scotland. The countless rivers littering the Central Belt permitted the development of these mills and movement away from home-working handloom weavers. The force of the rivers could be utilised to power the mill machinery and this practice only became more commonplace with the new craze for cotton as time ticked into the nineteenth century.

Easily the most renowned were the New Lanark mills. To the south-west of Glasgow following the River Clyde inland, a concentration of mills alongside the Clyde grew into a small town of manufacturing activity. Founded in 1785, they became not only the largest of their type in the world but also a benchmark for excellence in terms of efficiency and worker welfare. Workers lived, shopped and socialised on site, ensuring a familial community feel for all in the village.

The mills of the New Lanark World Heritage Site on the banks of the River Clyde.

There were even on-site schools for the children and the combined high living standards and productivity saw around 2,500 dedicated people living there with a strategy that rejected the accepted norm that treating workers badly was the best route to financial profit. It remains standing today as a World Heritage Site and one of Scotland's most thoughtfully presented and preserved visitor attractions.

Steam also entered the mix around this time, although Scotland was slow on the uptake and stuck with water power initially. However the Springfield Mill, steam-powered, arrived in Glasgow in 1792 and by the 1830s Glasgow was home to over 100 of them.

POWER TO THE PEOPLE

The city's marketing departments of today proudly boom that 'People Make Glasgow'. It's seen as the distinguisher, the asset that can't be contested and the draw that will keep bringing visitors back again and again. The friendly city, with a big heart. It's also a gentle dig at Edinburgh, but I'll not go there. Behind that handy PR slogan, however, comes a need for deeper analysis of the Glaswegian. Adjectives including honest, hardy, blunt, direct, fiery, cheeky, brave, unapologetic and industrious all spring quickly to mind. Big personalities. There's a lot of laughter to be heard in a Glasgow conversation and Glaswegians love a good joshing, love poking fun and love, usually, getting some of it poked back. We don't take a lot of things very seriously, yet take some things very seriously indeed. There's an almost confrontationally gruff side there, yet you'll struggle to find stronger empathy and solidarity, or more generous souls. So where do these paradoxes come from?

I'm going to propose that they go all the way back to the days of early industry, where hard graft met for maybe the first time – certainly on an organised level – with a rigid insistence on fairness. The Calton weavers were a case in point, inhabitants of a village just outside Glasgow at the time, which is now part of the East End. In 1787, they went on strike. Over the coming centuries, Glasgow would see plenty more as workers dug in, protesting against perceived unfairness, and powerful trade unions and left-leaning political viewpoints were cemented into society. By that year there were well over 50,000 weavers in Glasgow and it employed more workers than any other industry. They were well-paid workers too, highly regarded and skilled and earning in the region of £100 a year, in a century when demand had risen strongly worldwide. But the move to mechanisation and cheaper, unskilled, labour had driven down wages for the handweavers, and they took to the streets in protest. Organised marches and industrial action had a long and difficult road ahead of it but in these early times, violence and chaos were almost inevitable. Seven thousand protesting weavers descended on Glasgow Green, where fires were lit and law enforcement overwhelmed. Those workers who did not join the protest and show solidarity were turned on, their looms destroyed. The military were called in and three protesters were killed, with many more injured. This was the first major industrial dispute in Scotland.

The issue rumbled on as migration from rural areas to Glasgow continued at pace, and a surge of Irish workers arrived too, to the extent that by the mid-nineteenth century a quarter of Glasgow's population was Irish. The end of the Napoleonic Wars in the early 1800s brought more hungry mouths back home to Britain also. With only so many jobs to go round, the quality of life fell while wages and social problems went the other way. The eighteenth century closed with a sad chord for this industry that could not last, and the search was on for the next big thing.

TOBACCO

I remember fondly the time – in my Strathclyde University days in 2004 – when the ban on smoking in internal places was introduced in Scotland. The really quite shocking and sudden ability to breathe freely in bars and restaurants without feeling the stifling grip of trapped second-hand smoke or the luxury to not inflict numerous washes on clothes to rid them of the stale stench for days afterwards ... it was quite something. It was the latest firm step in shunning smoking in our society. It's hard then to reflect on how this must have been in reverse, when interest in tobacco took the world by storm.

A plant that was generally chewed or smoked via a pipe (cigarettes came later), it was the product that really launched Glasgow as an economic player in the world game, and brought staggering wealth to a handful of individuals who are still referred to as 'the Tobacco Lords'. Links would strengthen over the eighteenth century with Virginia in particular as trade flourished with America, and Scotland could now fully reap the economic benefits of Empire membership.

Glasgow became the first entry point into Europe for voyagers across the Atlantic, with goods then able to springboard further afield. From around 1740, Glasgow gradually but firmly became the epicentre of Britain's tobacco trade, and opportunities for canny businessmen were plentiful as around half of Europe's tobacco imports came in via Scotland's west coast. The Glasgow Chamber of Commerce became only the second in the world in 1783 – behind New York – and became something of a members' club for local businessmen keen on formally co-ordinating manufacturing and trade. The French monarchy even granted Glasgow a monopoly as the sole port of importation for France's sizeable territories in 1747. So were born the famous Tobacco Lords, and to this day streets in the Merchant City in the heart of town are named after some of them – Ingram, Glassford and Buchanan to name but three. The billionaires of their time, they led an almost aristocratic lifestyle in their private lives, while presiding over fleets, workers and tobacco stores professionally. Their homes were decadent, their clothing striking and their manner dominant. Several were also extremely generous when it came to giving back to the city that had given so much to them. Let's take a closer look at a few.

First up, John Glassford and Archibald Ingram. Connected through marriage, their business successes in the mid-eighteenth century were remarkable. With tobacco stores in America and a vast fleet of vessels at their disposal, they rose to the top of the tree throughout the peak times of tobacco trading, stealing a march on much of their future competition. They would go on to own various plantations in Virginia and Maryland, and Glassford especially would be regarded as one of Europe's greatest ever merchants. He could have been earning as much as £500,000 a year, a staggering amount for the times. With his wealth he would purchase numerous mansions in and around Glasgow as well as be an active backer of most of the manufacturing businesses across town. Ingram became Lord Provost and was a key financial backer of the Foulis Academy of the Arts before his death in 1770. The Academy, thought to be the first school housing fine arts in Glasgow, died off shortly after him.

Today, Glasgow's Gallery of Modern Art is among the city's most visited cultural attractions, dominant in Royal Exchange Square in the heart of town. Still a majestically grand building, it was once the home of William Cunninghame, one of the greatest tobacco beneficiaries. Ayrshire-born, he worked his way up within an import business, overseeing operations in Virginia and eventually taking control of the business for himself. Even when the Tobacco Lords were met with the devastating American Revolution (more to come on that), Cunninghame was savvy enough to have hoarded large quantities of tobacco before the price rocketed, which he was then able to sell on at vast profit as the war dragged on and the imperial gravy train ground to a permanent halt. Those profits likely built the gallery in 1780, which is still instantly recognisable today as the building backdropping the iconic Duke of Wellington statue. Hero of the Napoleonic Wars, his famously stern personality is joshed in the most Glasgow way possible with his statue being perpetually topped by a cheeky traffic cone. Occasional token gesture attempts by the City Council to remove it only result in great joy being taken by the next bold passer-by in rectifying the situation. The cone stays.

The cone-topped Duke of Wellington statue, sentinel outside the Gallery of Modern Art.

The great Mitchell Library, founded by the merchant Stephen Mitchell, is another lasting legacy. The largest reference library in Europe, it's been a place of learning for generations, and remains so today. Grand townhouses and churches would have been popping up ten a penny in these goldrush times as the still fairly modest town began to swell westwards, with population figures surging from around 20,000 to 200,000 in just a few decades. Whether generous, credibility-raising or just to get on good terms with the man upstairs, constructing centres of religion seemed to be another popular means of money spending for the nouveau riche among Glasgow's society. The church at St Andrew's in the Square was commissioned by the Tobacco Lords and still stands as an eye-catching place of celebration, just off High Street. I've attended a very memorable wedding there myself. Aside from the cathedral, St Andrew's Parish Church is the oldest active religious centre in the city. Constructed in 1756 behind the bustling Saltmarket, it is one of the known camping spots for the passing-through Jacobite armies that were met with such an underwhelming welcome. Just around the corner, St Andrew's by the Green is from the same period and is the oldest surviving Episcopalian church in the nation, going on to cater to a largely Presbyterian Glaswegian audience right up to 1975. Something is clear and undeniable – tobacco money built the foundations of the city and the society that we know and still recognise hundreds of years later.

Behind all that wealth generation inevitably lies something sinister in the shadows. For the workers that made these plantations, that put in the physical graft, were slaves. Glasgow was a key marker in the triangular trade routes between Africa and the Americas whereby slaves were plucked from West Africa, sent across the Atlantic to work in Virginia and the Caribbean, with the ships then returning the finished tobacco products (and in-demand extras such as rum, cotton and sugar) to Glasgow, and then returning manufactured goods back to Africa as payment for the next round of slaves. The moneymen would have overseen all of this, caring not for the rights of the African workers or the abhorrent and immoral nature of the cycle. To them the cheap labour would have made simple sense and the ability to re-export tobacco products

The striking St Andrew's in the Square just off High Street on the edges of the East End.

from Glasgow into wider Europe at enormous profit was all that mattered. During this century between 1 and 2 million slaves made that traumatising journey, and their treatment is thought to have worsened as demand rose and landowner profits improved. To its credit, the Gallery of Modern Art does not shirk from this shameful connection, with an exhibit documenting the story of the building and Cunninghame's unsettling road to riches is a key part of any visit. The past cannot be changed but it is not a chapter that Glaswegians are proud of and there has been increasing speculation that some of those famous Merchant City streets could be due for appropriate name changes in the not too distant future.

BEER

Tobacco wasn't the only vice creeping into society at large, as the courting began in the long and winding relationship between Glasgow and beer. Tennent's Lager is the nation's favourite these days, ubiquitous in every bar and hoarding an untouchably dominant percentage of the market share for pale lager. It was first produced by the Drygate (later Wellpark) Brewery in 1885, which sits close to the cathedral and Necropolis graveyard and it is thought to have been the first lager to be produced in the United Kingdom and the first draught lager in the world. The Tennent's company itself, though, was formed in 1740 by Hugh and Robert Tennent, the latest in a succession of family brewers, but the first to brew the stuff commercially. Brewing on the banks of the Molendinar may have gone considerably further back to medieval times, when stout and ale would have been the order of the day, and may also make them the oldest still-existing business of any kind in Scotland. The end of the eighteenth century saw shipments sent to America. High-strength, made-to-last brews were exported for the long crossing of the Atlantic as Tennent's became international, and the brand continues to be one of the most immediately recognisable in the land.

Revolution in the Air

The American War of Independence (1775–83) brought a swift end to this wealth accumulation and many, John Glassford included, saw their fortunes collapse. Growing animosity in Britain's American colonies towards the Empire, largely based on taxes levelled on them by the British government, escalated into armed conflict in 1775. Backed by the French as of 1778, this became a full-on international war as British control of their lucrative American colonies began to slip away. A series of battles raged along the eastern seaboard of what are now the United States, with both sides suffering high losses and minimal progress. The definitive victory came in October 1771 at the Battle of Yorktown, where combined American and French forces trapped and forced the surrender of opposing redcoats. Military momentum had by this point swung away from the British and the Treaty of Paris recognised American independence in 1783.

Tobacco did in part contribute to the colonisers' downfall. The Americans used the valuable product as collateral in the loan they secured for French support and, on securing their new independence, it became their route out of debts accumulated for the conflict and the basis for a new economy as trade with Europe continued, only without British control. Bypassed and reeling, Glasgow's economy faced the challenge of reinventing itself again, something that history reveals Glaswegians to have been very proficient at.

ENTER THE BANKERS

With growth comes money, and with money comes bankers. Scotland has a long banking history and it was arguably the most developed in the world up until the 1820s. Following the Jacobite hostilities, a period of relative calm came over Britain and opportunities to peacefully carry out business started anew. The moneymen, hitherto concentrated in Edinburgh, started to pop up in Glasgow as an increasing number of merchants sought finance close to home; those involved in the tobacco trade most of all.

Fast-forwarding slightly, the City of Glasgow Bank came on to the scene in 1839 and accumulated more than 100 branches in the following decades. These new Glasgow-based banks were perhaps seen as offering something a little less conservative to those in the capital, keen no doubt to capitalise on the prospect of untapped global opportunity that had been breezing in on the Atlantic air. Scandal was never far away, however, and it was to crash completely on the revelation that it had been accumulating massive liabilities thanks to the side investments of its directors. Jail followed for them, with the vast majority of the bank's shareholders facing ruin, and a city-wide financial crisis unfolded.

There were more successful, less fraudulent endeavours, as evidenced in 1749 by what began as the Ship Bank and would go on to merge much later with the Bank of Scotland. Its notes evocatively depicted a ship in full sail. Quickly taking a competitive position against the Bank of Scotland (a separate, Edinburgh-based institution at the time), it established branches in both cities and started to return impressive balance sheets. Although rocked by the American Revolution, the bank still performed very strongly in the closing decades of the 1700s as trade became focussed instead on the West Indies. Accompanying the city's economy as the linen and tobacco trades declined, it would go on to become the Glasgow and Ship Bank in 1836 and then the Union Bank of Scotland in 1843. It was to be in this century that Glasgow upped its game once more.

3

THE NINETEENTH CENTURY AND THE ARRIVAL OF HEAVY INDUSTRY

## SHIPBUILDING – THE BEGINNINGS

Glasgow was the shipbuilder to the world, with the Clyde and its shipyards the very epicentre. Amid a constant cacophony of noise and hard labour, a riot of construction of ships big and small would have made the riverside among the most dynamic workplaces on earth. The world's factory, it has been called. This remained so until the 1970s and the dire economic decline that we'll get to later. But the explosion in Scotland's fascination with seafaring travel really began with the start of Queen Victoria's reign in 1837. Road and rail were slow and unreliable and long-distance travel and trade around Britain was simply best done over water, even if that meant navigating some treacherous stretches of coastline in often violent weather conditions. I'll talk more about this in the Transport chapter but, suffice to say, Scotland's deep historic bond with the seas only strengthened through the Empire years. It's no surprise, then, that Glasgow seized the central role in sharing the fruits of that bond with the world. Let's explore some of the most impressive feats.

The Cunard Steam Ship Company was a prime example of Scottish business excellence. Going on to become one of the most famous shipping companies in the world, it had Scottish entrepreneurial vision at its heart. Scots Sir George Burns and Robert Napier aligned their shipping and engineering expertise with owner Samuel Cunard to create a pioneering fleet as we entered the age of steam. Transatlantic passenger voyages were now possible on the paddle steamer *Britannia* from 1840. They would go on to build the *Queen Mary* and both *Queen Elizabeths* and they started producing steel vessels in the 1860s, one of which was the RMS *Servia*, the first to have a Royal Mail contract. And the *Persia* was launched in 1855. She was 350ft long, making her the largest vessel on the planet at the time, and was prominent on the seas until 1863.

Similarly, the Anchor Line company was shuttling passengers across the Atlantic from 1856, with Scots departing to new world adventures in huge numbers. Not built to be extravagant or overly luxurious, the company's reputation was one of affordability and accessibility for ordinary citizens. Their marketing material is a thing of beauty, with bright, bold posters beaming an image of adventure. Proudly Scottish by design, not to mention employing hundreds of local Clydesiders on each ship, they pitched at the local markets successfully while also enticing American travellers with romantic images of faraway Scotland, ancestral home to so many from across the pond. Picture loch-side stags posing before mountainous backdrops, amusingly not dissimilar to today's VisitScotland promotional fare. Their early motto had been 'Secure Amid Perils', a dubious claim given that more than twenty of their ships were lost at sea, but such were the risks of early ocean-bound travel on this scale. Their plentiful fleet was constructed out of Meadowside in Partick and would go on to be consumed by the Cunard Line in 1911, though it continued to operate successfully for decades until the last of its ships was withdrawn from service in the 1980s.

The *Comet* was the world's first seagoing steam ship, launched from Port Glasgow in 1812. It first provided a passenger service between Glasgow and Greenock. Setting trends that others speedily followed, the route was extended north to Helensburgh and then the Crinan Canal and the Oban to Inverness route. Its boiler was built by David Napier, who would go on to make a huge personal contribution to Glasgow's shipbuilding heritage as an engine designer. His cousin, Robert Napier of Cunard fame, is still regarded as the 'father' of Clyde shipbuilding. His shipyards produced numerous famous vessels and he provided the facilities and training for so many of the other great visionaries who masterminded the industry.

Campbeltown native David Colville was among the first to see the transition from iron to steel in the shipbuilding industry and his pioneering open-hearth furnace technique was the start of an extraordinary legacy that began in the 1860s and spanned over a century. There was also the Glaswegian marine engineer John Elder, who created the compound engine in 1854, a design that massively reduced fuel consumption for sea vessels, naturally increasing their potential range by 30 to 40 per cent. And that's just for starters, I'll be returning to shipbuilding shortly.

OTHER INDUSTRIAL ACTIVITY AND TRADES

Locally, trade continued at pace. The long-running Paddy's Market was set up by Irish immigrants from the 1820s as a means of job creation in the East End, this around the time that Glasgow's population surpassed that of Edinburgh. With the previous century's trend of moving west and away from the traditional heart of local economic activity in the east continuing, this market became a second-hand Aladdin's cave of affordable products. The potato famine of the mid-1800s saw it swell further and ultimately it would spend the next centuries being moved around the city by authorities trying to keep it in check. 'The Briggait', Glasgow's old fish market, was built in 1873 and the Chamber of Commerce and Manufacture continued to champion commercial interests city-wide throughout the century.

The final decades of it saw increased everyday demand for exotic goods such as fruit and vegetables. Greengrocer extraordinaire Sir Malcolm Campbell was perhaps the biggest facilitator and did more than his share for improving public health by importing the likes of bananas, melons and grapes for consumption by the city's growing population. Meanwhile, the Scottish staple, whisky, had a local source in the form of Auchentoshan Distillery. Founded in 1800 in the Kilpatrick Hills north-west of the city, it is still going strong today and has very recently been joined by an even closer option for whisky connoisseurs in the form of the Clydeside Distillery, which is within walking distance of the city centre on the riverside.

Some of these great entrepreneurial minds of the times took their business visions global. Sir Thomas Lipton is still a household name in the world of tea; the St Rollox Chemical Works was the largest in the world during this century, the product of the vision of the aforementioned Charles Tennant; the scientist William Cullen, with a background in explosives, took his expertise to oversee the lucrative mines of South Africa. Massive progress was made in the field of gas thanks to Glaswegian Dugald Clerk who, in the 1870s, began pioneering work to harness gas as a fuel. With engines his primary focus, he also pushed for the use of gas as a source of power for heating and lighting. Even within the military, visionary minds from Glasgow rose to the top. Sir John Moore led the British Army – shortly before Arthur Wellesley, the Duke of Wellington, arrived on the scene – in the early stages of the Napoleonic Wars. And Sir Colin Campbell was a hugely respected field marshal of British forces in Asia in the mid-century. Glaswegians travel well, make no mistake.

The Saracen Ironworks Foundry became one of Scotland's industrial powerhouses, a business that started in Saracen Lane in the Gallowgate in the 1850s but would relocate ultimately to Possilpark in the north-west of Glasgow in the 1870s. Producing ornamental-style ironworks (mainly for exporting), the range of their potential products was huge, from domestic appliances to public railings, gates and fountains. On a huge 14-acre site that included railway access, the population of the newly named Possilpark rocketed from barely double digits to more than 10,000 in the space of twenty years. Despite its rapid growth in the closing decades of the century, the decline of the Empire, competition from the wider world and movements in demand away from iron ensured the foundry did not continue its remarkable success into the 1900s.

These are just a handful of examples, hopefully painting a picture of a city that had really found its foothold. The sounds, the smells, the energy ... can you feel it? Producing over half of Britain's massive shipping output, a quarter of the world's locomotives and having created head-spinning productivity, Glasgow adopted its now oft-repeated and undeniable title, 'the Second City of the Empire'.

SETTING GLASGOW IN STONE

One of the first things modern-day visitors to the city tend to note is Glasgow's diverse skyline. Architecturally eclectic in its remarkable range, the mix of old and new is bold and intriguing and undoubtedly among the key assets in the armoury. This owes much to the architects of the nineteenth century, who created buildings that not only caught the eye but that could withstand the perennially damp conditions of the west of Scotland.

Alexander 'Greek' Thomson is most worthy of this praise. If, like many, you've ever noted the enduring Victorian mood that lingers throughout the city, that is largely down to his legacy. Born in 1817 in Balfron, north of the city, Thomson began his architecture apprenticeship in the 1830s and soon identified a love for the Greek style. Majestic columns, stage-like podiums and sweeping horizontal lines gave us buildings that would have been well-suited to gladiator movies and there were some obvious Roman, Egyptian and Middle Eastern influences in there too. Bringing that north to Glasgow must have raised many an eyebrow, but bring it he did in the form of numerous churches, terraces, tenement housing and even a magnificent urban villa, Holmwood, which remains under the care of the National Trust for Scotland in the South Side. And perhaps what is most impressive in Thomson's contribution is the sustainability of it. Although some of his buildings have sadly slipped away due to human negligence, the city is still littered with his maker's mark. The striking St Vincent Street Church in the city centre is perhaps my favourite but he changed the appearance and tone of Glasgow completely during the 1850s and '60s, inspiring plenty of his peers as well. A highly religious and seemingly very serious man, of the Presbyterian manner, his no-nonsense approach not only stood the test of time but swept up worldwide recognition and influence long after his passing in 1875.

Numerous others left their mark in this century of construction. Local boy David Hamilton designed the Hutcheson's Hospital in 1802, the Nelson's Column in Glasgow Green in 1806 and the Royal Exchange in 1829. The latter is, of course, a repurposing of the Tobacco Lord William Cunninghame's mansion. In 1841 he also built the stunning 191 Ingram Street in the Merchant City, which today is the remarkably extravagant Corinthian Bar. Hamilton's understudy, Charles Wilson, picked up the baton and designed large chunks of the West End including affluent Park Circus overlooking Kelvingrove Park, a district with clear shades of Edinburgh's New Town to its look and feel. The building boom accelerated in the 1870s with another Glaswegian, James Sellars, profiting through the St Andrew's Halls and then the Victoria Infirmary and what would become the House of Fraser department store on Buchanan Street. One of

The beautiful South Side villa of Holmwood House, one of Alexander Thomson's masterpieces.

The eye-catching St Vincent Street Church in the city centre.

many influenced by Alexander Thomson, he also worked on commissions for the Saracen Foundry. As for the most famous Glasgow architect of them all, Charles Rennie Mackintosh, I'll be returning to him later in more detail.

The legacy of the aforementioned Tobacco Lord, Stephen Mitchell, was the superb Mitchell Library. Initially located in Ingram Street in the city centre in 1877, it moved first to Miller Street then to Charing Cross. A neoclassical design by William Brown Whitie, it is one of the most recognisable in the city, and is particularly impressive when lit up at night. Supplementing any remnants from the times of the Tobacco Lords, the majority of what modern-day locals and visitors associate with Glasgow was built in this century and the early decades of the next. In the 1820s what would become pretty Blythswood Square in the city centre also took the curious step of mimicking the New Town style seen in Edinburgh (even a broken clock ... etc, etc). The Kibble Palace – the giant glasshouse at the heart of the Botanic Gardens – was constructed in 1873 and remains one of the main points of interest in the West End, with the Botanics having opened to the public in 1891. Its warm, humid and welcoming air pulls in visitors of all ages keen on being whisked off to the Tropics and away from the grey Scottish skies and relentless sideways rain.

The Templeton Carpet Factory at Calton was completed in 1892 in a spectacularly bold exterior Italian design to match that of the magnificent Doge's Palace in Venice. And its neighbour the Doulton Fountain, which stands sentinel outside the People's Palace in Glasgow Green, arrived in 1888, giving that corner of the otherwise unremarkable park a touch of architectural class. An intricate terracotta design that saluted Queen Victoria and the seemingly limitless reach of the Empire, the fountain remains the city's most impressive. The factory itself was one of Britain's busiest in its heyday and the building now hosts offices, apartments and the West Brewery. I lived in the building myself once upon a time and take it from me, there are few things more satisfying than being able to step outside your apartment door, pop in the lift and emerge into a top-class bar for a pint with your slippers on. A Glaswegian Heart and a German Head is their motto, and its patrons approve.

Adjacent to them, and the heart of Glasgow Green, sits the much-loved People's Palace. Inclusiveness is central to Glasgow's culture scene. Most museums are free to enter and education is accessible to all who have an interest. This mindset possibly goes back to the final years of the 1800s when debate raged over whether the working classes would benefit from access to Glasgow's wealth of cultural assets. Opening in 1898, the People's Palace was established with the view that indeed they should. A social space in every sense, it was a museum, yes, but also a reading and recreation area and music venue. It tells the ups and downs story of Glaswegians from 1750 to the present day, covering housing, socialising, politics and more. Another striking red sandstone structure designed by Alexander Beith McDonald, it also long housed an array of tropical plant life in the connected Winter Gardens glasshouse.

The city's plethora of sandstone is worth a closer look. The stuff is everywhere, often setting a uniform appearance to lengthy residential streets or presenting a welcoming glow to our public buildings, in either blonde or red. Quarried in and around the city starting in the eighteenth century, the blonde variety dates from the Carboniferous period with large quantities coming from nearby Giffnock and Bishopbriggs. The red, meanwhile, dates from the Permian period and was shipped into the city as demand grew by the rail networks of the late nineteenth century, generally from Ayrshire and Dumfriesshire in Scotland's south-west. The general rule being that red buildings were likely constructed post-1890, the blonde pre-1890. Possessing higher iron content, the red variety proved more resistant to the elements and has endured better than the older blonde equivalents. The sheer quantities being extracted from the south-west also made it cheaper than the increasingly depleted local quarries and saw it shipped nationwide and even to America.

The People's Palace and Doulton Fountain set within Glasgow Green.

The City Chambers, the very epicentre of Glasgow, was built starting in 1883 under the instruction of Paisley architect William Young. The regal and intricate design draws on plenty of Italian influence too, with domed cupolas, pillars and statues booming status and power down upon George Square. The interior is a marble maze that screams opulence, topped by the Banqueting Hall. It was opened by Queen Victoria in 1888 and remains very much in active use as the headquarters of the City Council. Any visitor to the city should book themselves a place on one of the free walking tours of the interior, which for some reason too few folk know about. For the nearby High Street, however, times have not been so kind and many of its historic buildings are no longer with us. One resilient hanger-on, though, is the beautiful former British Linen Bank building at No. 215. A Category B listed building dating to 1895, plans are afoot, at the time of writing, to restore and repurpose it, potentially as an art exhibition and event space.

As for Glasgow University, it made its permanent move from the city centre to the West End in 1870. Overcrowding and general decline had driven many west, away from the High Street, and the university joined the trend by selling up the land to the Glasgow Union Railway Company and migrating its sizable campus to Gilmorehill, a distance of around 3 miles. A striking design was created by Sir George Gilbert Scott, adopting an eerie Gothic Revival style and all-seeing spire tower for its primary building. Very much at odds with the vast majority of the architectural styles on display across Glasgow, it remains arguably the most instantly recognisable today. Needless to say, however, it received its share of criticism and Alexander Thomson for one was clearly not a fan. With his own iconic styling preferences shunned in favour of his English peer's Gothic vision – that clearly took inspiration from Oxford and Cambridge – Thomson went so far as to deliver a paper to the Glasgow Architectural Society titled 'An inquiry as to the appropriateness of the Gothic Style for the proposed buildings for the University of Glasgow, with some remarks upon Mr Scott's plans'. If ever you needed a dictionary definition for 'passive aggressive', Alex there is your man. In any case, it seems likely that chat may have been a little awkward for all concerned. With objections noted and ignored, though, it became the largest public building in Britain since Westminster Palace had been constructed a decade before, another with which it shares an inescapable

The Glasgow University campus at Gilmorehill.

resemblance. Watching over Kelvingrove Park, its evocative and almost fantastical appearance have seen it inspire many a creative mind.

THE GLASGOW BOYS

The 1880s saw the informal coming together of a group of radical young painters with attitude – and no shortage of talent. Flying the flag for modernism and contemporary art of their time, they railed against the more Establishment artistic styles to more thoughtfully capture the character of Glasgow and Scotland, with their works remaining favourites of city visitors to this day. Often involving sketches directly in front of their subject matter, the artists took inspiration from styles being rolled out across the world, particularly Continental Europe and Japan. The focus was on realism and naturalism – painting outdoors a lot of the time, striving to capture things exactly as they were. Real people doing real things in a way that could be almost physically touched, often inspiring melancholy and deep reflection from the audience. James Guthrie, James Paterson and John Lavery were among the leaders of the sizeable group that numbered around twenty, all based in and around the city. Backed by some of Glasgow's wealthy elite at the time, they forged a slice of the city's cultural history for themselves and their work can be enjoyed best at Kelvingrove Art Gallery and Museum, where over sixty of their pieces are on display in their own room.

Not to be outshone, the Glasgow Girls were a similarly minded group of designers and artists from an overlapping period, although they would not be referred to as a collective until the mid-twentieth century. Boasting Margaret and Frances Macdonald in their ranks – the former married to, and professionally aligned with, the iconic Charles Rennie Mackintosh – they were largely students at the School of Art who thrived on the unprecedent creative spaces available in the city.

CITY LIVING

For a land famously blessed with an inexhaustible supply of liquid from the heavens, it seems strange to think that decent drinking water was not something that could always be taken for granted in Glasgow. The search for quality water was taken up by William Harley around 1800 when he took a step back from his cloth manufacturing business to set up Blythswood Estate. Sourcing and distributing water taken from natural springs, he provided clean drinking water on an as-yet-unseen scale to the city dwellers. With its demand obvious, Glasgow then set up its first water company in 1807. Harley, incidentally, then turned his attention to public baths, which he set up on his estate and which gives the neighbouring present-day Bath Street its name. Trendy Blythswood Square still exists on that street. Public baths (or Steamies) became commonplace in the grimy times of the Industrial Revolution when clothes and bodies were in near-constant need of cleaning. They started as far back as 1732 on Glasgow Green when women would take their family bundles for a good handwringing. It became something of a social event, to the extent that the term 'talk of the steamie' was born, as local news and goings-on were dissected between washes. This community trend lasted right up to the 1980s. Formal bath clubs, meanwhile, started with the Arlington in 1871 which catered to the demand from those living around Charing Cross. The stylish venue retains its Victorian air and now boasts a 21m pool, saunas and hot tubs, remaining open to members over 150 years later.

Regulating the water supply for the city's growing population came in to play in the nineteenth century when the local rivers and reservoirs were utilised. The quality, however, left a lot to be desired, with disease and illness commonplace as a result. The cholera epidemic of the late 1840s was particularly damning, and lethal. For the first time on any sort of scale, cemeteries began to appear across the city as a result. The Necropolis overlooking the cathedral is the best known and holds the remains of the city's rich and famous who died between 1832 and 1867. Three other cemeteries without religious affiliation were established in the mid-century.

As already suggested, overcrowding was also increasingly becoming an issue as Glasgow had become a beacon for families in Britain and Ireland looking for work. For context, the population in 1750 was 32,000, by 1830 it was close to 200,000 and by 1870 it was approximately 500,000. Unsurprisingly, the city's infrastructure struggled badly during this period, with quality of life often extremely poor. It was not until 1855 that a permanent solution to the water issue specifically was found. Loch Katrine sits in the Trossachs well to the north of Glasgow and just to the east of the more famous Loch Lomond, and its soft and pure offerings remain the water source for the city to this day. Following a bill passed by Queen Victoria, a remarkable engineering project was undertaken to successfully pump water across 26 miles of aqueduct and using 4 miles of piping. Navigating challenging terrain, this pipeline was completed by hand and brought a limitless amount of high-quality water to homes and businesses across town. In Kelvingrove Park, the striking French-Gothic Stewart Memorial Fountain salutes this extraordinary endeavour. A new sewerage system was constructed around the same time and the Western Infirmary was built as a teaching hospital as part of the university. These efforts combined saw the population's health improve drastically.

The Stewart Memorial Fountain im Kelvingrove Park.

But the city overseers had to go further. The City Improvement Act of 1866 outlined a wider plan to improve living standards and rectify the high crime rates, overcrowding and wealth inequality. Slum housing was to be demolished, streets were to be redesigned and building regulations that targeted overcrowding were established. An unprecedented and ambitious overhaul of the city's housing was under way. Success was far from an overnight reality but by the turn of the century quality tenement flats were being constructed in large numbers across Glasgow, part of a lasting housing landscape that has endured wonderfully. Slums were replaced by multi-room housing that had running water and even, wait for it, inside toilets. In most instances, private landlords and builders were permitted to build on the newly cleared sites, but on the condition that they met quality standards. Tenement life has been central to my own domestic outlook and the communal nature of urban living, tucked away in a small corner of a sandstone jungle, is still something that gives me an enormously comforting sense of familiarity. The typical tenement 'close' is a little less convivial these days of course – with people more inclined to mind their own business – but chatting to neighbours on the stairs, fighting over the last of the garden's spare laundry line and bemoaning the state of the shared chimney flue are all frequent goings on in my day-to-day. I wouldn't have it any other way.

4

THE TWENTIETH CENTURY – A TIME OF EXTREMES

By now Glasgow's most prominent industry, shipbuilding continued its dynamic and confident journey into the new century. In 1907, the largest crane in the world, the Titan, was completed to sit on the banks of the Clyde. The world's first electrically powered cantilever crane, it stood at a whopping 150ft and underlined the ambition of the John Brown & Company shipyard on which it was built. Its extraordinary lifting capacity would go on to aid in the construction of many of the finest ships of the century including the *Queen Mary,* which was launched into the Clyde in 1934. Over 1,000ft long, it was the largest liner ever built and was a welcome high point in the belt-tightening times brought by the Great Depression, when shipyards suddenly lay idle and workers faced the dole. In 1913, the staggering output from the Clyde yards totalled around 750,000 tonnes, but this had plummeted to around 10,000 by 1933, and the *Queen Mary* lay in a partially complete state for years as the banks blocked any further investment. It took a government subsidy to get it over the line. In the end, the local and international fanfare and excitement for the launch was unprecedented. It was the biggest, the fastest, the most luxurious and it was built by the best, at John Brown's shipyard. She would carry 5,000 passengers and crew, held twenty decadent public rooms, a car park, gymnasium and numerous spa baths. The kitchens could produce 20,000 meals a day, making the five-day Atlantic crossings an experience of pioneering luxury and extravagance. Truly a feat to behold. She was retired in 1967 after 1,001 Atlantic crossings and now serves as a floating hotel in California. The all-important Titan crane, meanwhile, also overlooked the creation of the *Queen Elizabeth* and *Queen Elizabeth II* and is now a tourist attraction in the form of a shipbuilding museum and, amusingly, a bungee jump venue.

Many of the ships being churned out in the lead up to the First World War were commandeered from passenger and trade duties to join the war efforts that so influenced the first half of the twentieth century. The Cunard-built *Aquitania* was launched in 1913 amid more public delirium, it too being the largest liner in the world of its time, at over 900ft. Having barely dipped its toe, it was also quickly enlisted as a troop transport and hospital ship in the First World War, and again in the Second.

Throughout the Great War, and onwards, Glasgow was the undoubted centre of British shipbuilding. The northern powerbase was employing 70,000 workers across 19 yards as the war began and battles for control of the seas raged to unprecedented levels. Decades later, the *Queen Elizabeth* and *Queen Mary* were lauded with the greatest of praise from Winston Churchill himself, who observed that their presence shortened the Second World War by over a year. Not all of the Clyde-built vessels were so fortunately decorated, however. The *Lusitania* was comfortably the largest ship in the world when it launched from Clydebank in 1906 and, although also requisitioned for war duties, served principally as a transatlantic passenger service. Tragically, she was sunk by a U-boat torpedo off the Irish coast in 1915, with hundreds of casualties. Then there's the *Waverley*, launched in 1899, which served in both wars before being sunk during the panicked evacuation of troops from Dunkirk in 1940. Three hundred people went down with her. Fortunately, another *Waverley* was created after the war and served as a paddle steamer and pleasure craft on the Clyde. She's still going, too, and ferrying visitors from the city to the holiday hotspots of old on the coast. On a day trip to Bute recently, I endured the squalls of west of Scotland weather to have a lovely day on the island before returning home for dinner. Passengers can duck below to observe the engine room in action or return the salutes of waving landlubbers as she steams along in tribute to a fine legacy. Although running costs have almost spelled an end to such adventures, funding rescue packages have always come through and this is one tradition this Glaswegian hopes never dies.

I'll be returning to the wars in a later chapter but the shipbuilding heart of Scotland was an obvious target for German bombers and, in 1941, Clydebank to the west of Glasgow was near-destroyed by Luftwaffe payloads. Hundreds were killed, thousands injured and only a handful of the town's buildings were left standing. While damaging the munitions and manufacturing capacity of Clydeside, the attack merely served to strengthen the local and national resolve to persevere with the war effort. Glasgow itself was fortunate not to suffer such a fate, as was the Titan crane, which remained stoically and defiantly standing downriver from the surrounding carnage.

Following the war, decimated navies and merchant fleets turned their eye on Glasgow as the task of rebuilding began, though it was to be a short-lived boom. The transatlantic fleet had been decimated, with those ships still afloat in long overdue need of repairs. Passenger sailings in the once majestic journeys from Glasgow to New York were scaled back dramatically. Competition from Asia, particularly Japan, and then the decision of the British government to privatise shipbuilding in the 1960s ensured a permanent decline. In response to the obvious crisis, the British government created the Upper Clyde Shipbuilders consortium in 1968, which saw the amalgamation of five of the shipbuilding firms, backed by the government as a minority holder. It failed in 1971 when the government refused further financial aid, a new crisis that triggered the famous 'work in'. This 'anti-strike' saw workers continue to work on the backlog of shipping orders at the yards, without pay and under exemplary behaviour, with a view to shaming the government into providing support and to gather public sympathy. The latter objective was quickly achieved as large demonstrations of outrage at the potential job losses followed, with the clamour loud enough to force a rethink in London the following year. The yards would now be structured around two companies, the Govan Shipbuilders (formerly Fairfields) and Yarrow Shipbuilders at Scotstoun, with the government temporarily keeping these two yards afloat. The Conservative government under Margaret Thatcher would infamously go on to break this up, denationalising British Shipbuilders (formerly Govan Shipbuilders) in 1988. An army of highly experienced and skilled workers would lose their jobs, with the resulting widespread hatred of Thatcher eclipsing any I've seen towards a political leader in this country in my lifetime. Glasgow's proudest industry was finished.

OTHER INDUSTRY

In addition to the construction of ships to navigate the world, locomotive production also boomed further in the city in the first half of the century. The North British Locomotive Company, a combination of three Glasgow engineering companies, was formed in 1903 and became the largest builder in the world. It had produced 5,000 of them by the time the Great War began, at which point it turned to munitions. These giant beasts would be transported across land, hoisted up on the giant cranes and lowered on to the ships to turn dreams to reality for travellers and romantics everywhere. But the interwar downturn and the transition away from steam power to diesel engines proved too much. The previously unmatched quality of the engines was compromised by the growing market trend for this new fuel, not enough research had been done, supply chains elsewhere stole a march, quality standards fell and eventually the company went under in 1962 to mark the end of another era.

Car manufacturing too could be found in the form of Albion Motors and others. Originally based out of Scotstoun and in operation until 1980, Albion Motors produced private and commercial vehicles ranging from wagonettes to buses, and even 3-ton trucks during the First World War. Halley's Industrial Motors in Yoker was another to thrive at this time, by meeting the military demand for motor vehicles and becoming one of the leading manufacturers in Britain during the war years.

But engineering in Scotland took many forms and countless examples exist that saw companies and individuals excel in this century of extremes. William Beardmore & Co. was among the biggest employers in the country in the 1920s, with over 45,000 on the books. Although most renowned for its steel manufacturing in Parkhead and shipbuilding from Napier's shipyard in Dalmuir, the Beardmore Motor Company also produced cars and taxis and, from 1913, aircraft. In these early days of air travel, their planes themselves were not particularly successful, but their engines were. And there was William Douglas Weir, too. His company was among the top in the world for pumps and mechanical machinery for marine engines. Specialists in diversification, they moved into aircraft assembly and munitions to meet demand in the First World War, surviving the Depression and booming again from the surge in demand brought about by the Second World War. Let's not forget Rolls-Royce either, as the Hillington plant was producing 400 Merlin engines a week for Spitfire and Hurricane fighters in 1943. It's an exhaustive list.

It's time to look at John Logie Baird, whose work in the 1920s brought us the television. A local of Helensburgh and student of Glasgow University, his was a career fit for the screen as a series of whacky ideas eventually delivered him into the history books. During the First World War he had worked for the Clyde Valley Electrical Power Company but had landed himself in hot water after he 'borrowed' the electricity supply in the belief that he could use it to manufacture diamonds. The network may have crashed. There may have been an explosion. There may not have been any evidence of diamonds. He also failed, painfully I'd imagine, to create a cure for piles. Undeterred, he then created a waterproof sock that wasn't very waterproof and started an ill-fated jam business in Trinidad that was set upon, and his dreams carried off, by swarms of insects. We've all been there. Finally, he made the breakthrough when he achieved 'half-tone' television pictures in 1925 and would present the first demonstration of television to an audience in London the following year. In 1927, live television pictures were broadcast from London to Glasgow using a telephone line and then to New York using short-wave radio. The BBC first adopted his ideas in 1929 and he kept working on improving the experience for viewers right up until his death in 1946, by which time he'd achieved impressive results with colour television, too. I get the feeling he would have been good value at a dinner party.

City Development

Following the First World War, the powers that be in Glasgow boldly attempted their endless task to improve the lot of its people through improved housing and living facilities. From 1919 it was compulsory for local authorities to plan housing schemes, with the ambition being to build sustainable, cottage-style homes that offered garden space, access to sport areas and plentiful local amenities. National economic factors blocked some of this ambition and the inadequate supply of social housing caused a new wave of slums to develop across the city. Crime and violence flourished amid the unemployed and idle and this continued right up to the Second World War in 1939. But while the legends still linger about slum conditions in the likes of the Gorbals, Bridgeton, Kinning Park and more, there were areas where living standards were improving greatly and the interwar image of Glasgow as some sort of gangland bear pit was heavily exaggerated. What we can say is that the high-quality tenement flats built around the turn of the century have impressively stood the test of time and the ill-fated attempt to replicate them with lower-cost tenements in the 1930s often served only to provide drug dens and fertile land for the slumlords. Made of reconstituted stone, they were a backwards step in the city's construction journey, and brought on a lot of problems.

Post-Second World War, the economic challenges continued but the Bruce Plan of 1945 nonetheless proposed a wholesale reset of the city's layout. Although not accepted in its entirety, it ordered a motorway to be built to slice right through the city (as opposed to the more common approach of looping around it) and mass destruction of existing infrastructure commenced. A shocking mess must have been made but fortunately the preposterous idea of demolishing the City Chambers, Central Station and the School of Art was blocked. The overhaul also took up proposals from the 1949 Clyde Valley Regional Plan, most notably to shift much of Glasgow's populace to the New

Towns of East Kilbride, Cumbernauld and others across the Central Belt. This idea centred around eradicating the slums and offering the promise of there being a better quality of life to be had outwith the claustrophobic conditions of the big city. 'Schemes' such as at Easterhouse, Castlemilk and Drumchapel were established amid the construction of high-rise flats. The legacy of many of these grand plans are very much still alive today, for better or worse. The M8 motorway stabs into the concrete at Charing Cross and crosses the Clyde on the Kingston Bridge, loosely dividing what most now consider to be the West End and city centre.

There are many literary classics that delve deeply into the darker chapters of this century of struggle and despondency. *No Mean City* is known to all Glaswegians, the chilling depiction of interwar Glasgow and the dreaded razor gangs. Set in the Gorbals, perhaps the most notorious slum of them all, it is a wary journey to peer upon a life that none would choose and that all feared. More recently, the 2020 Booker Prize-winning novel *Shuggie Bain* tells the story of a young boy growing up in post-industrial Sighthill in the 1980s. It's a story of abuse, addiction, overcrowding, unfulfilled ambition and big-heartedness. So much of Glasgow and the Glaswegian come through, and it is surely one of the best chronicles of Glasgow life of its time. Oscar Marzaroli was a Scots-Italian photographer whose work captured day-to-day activities and 'real' people over a period of nearly forty years, with his most evocative work coming from 1960s Glasgow. Another photographer, Raymond Depardon, presented a haunting visual depiction of the run-down areas of the city in the 1980s. Commissioned by *Sunday Times Magazine*, his work,

titled simply 'Glasgow', captured a poverty-stricken side to a
once industrial powerhouse, trapped in a vicious economic
downturn. It's tragic, bleak and emotional.

This misery, toward which Scots too often tend to be drawn,
was, I must stress, not representative of the city as a whole. I
grew up in a one-bedroom tenement in the 1980s with what
would certainly be considered a working-class family income.
It wasn't tragic. Modest maybe, but it certainly wasn't an
impoverished lifestyle. We didn't walk around in fear for our
lives and Glasgow of that decade was not for the most part a
vast dangerous wasteland. However, undeniably, the extreme
economic divides from region to region in the city existed
then, as they still do now.

The city centre that we recognise today took shape with the
upgrade to the Merchant City in the 1970s and '80s. Decades
of decline, abandonment and poverty were washed away as
a massive regeneration project was undertaken. It is now one
of the most vibrant urban areas in Scotland, home to various
top-class restaurants, bars, shops and event venues. Not
since the times of the Tobacco Lords has its freshly gleaming
streets seen such a renewed bustle and class as street artists,
fine diners and high-end designer shoppers have turned it into
their playground. The youthful energy from the neighbouring
Strathclyde University students just about keeps the
pretentiousness at bay and a complementary mix of restored
Victorian decadence and futuristic international styles (with
lots of glass and artwork) ensures heads are constantly
elevated. Nearby Buchanan Street was pedestrianised in
1975 to embody the city's growing ambition to offer the best
shopping in the UK outside of London. The shrewd Hugh

Fraser was perhaps the biggest beneficiary in retail through the 1900s and his Glasgow legacy, House of Fraser, is still a dominant player on the high street scene. Its neighbour, the St Enoch Centre, houses more than eighty retail stores and was opened for business in 1989 as a shopping mall within a gigantic glass pyramid, at a cost exceeding £65 million. Recent plans are afoot to see it demolished in favour of the more traditional street grid system, though still with a focus on retail and hospitality. Despite the decline of high street shopping in recent times, the so-called 'Style Mile' encompassing Sauchiehall Street, Buchanan Street and Argyll Street is still a key element within the city's tourism strategy and local economy.

ESTABLISHING GLASGOW'S SOCIETY

The image and reputation of Glasgow as a dangerous, run-down place has proved an extremely hard one to shift, and I think it has its roots in the darker decades of the twentieth century. Spending my teenage years living in a commuter town not far from the city, I'd jump into it by train fairly frequently. Even within my friend circle at the time, the running joke was that you were taking your life into your hands as soon as you stepped off into Queen Street Station. Utter anything religious, speak ill of the wrong football team or just look at someone the wrong way and the knives would literally be out! Even today, friends from other parts of the United Kingdom still raise an eyebrow when I scoff at any safety fears about a night out in Glasgow. Of course, having worked through my university years in the city in the bars and nightclubs at all hours of the night, I can say with at least some authority that this reputation is inaccurate and outdated. But let's take a look at law and order in Glasgow.

The previous century had seen the early establishment of something resembling a co-ordinated and structured police force, indeed it has been described as the first modern-style municipal version in Britain. This grew to include 'watchmen', 'bobbies' and detectives. The image of Untouchable Sean Connery in police uniform scolding people and prodding them with his truncheon springs unavoidably to mind at this point. In 1912, the forces in the Partick and Govan burghs merged with the growing Glasgow force, though it was still divided into four geographic divisions. The fallout from the Great War put the growing police force to use as economic and social depression simmered. The gangs of the 1920s and '30s, whether inspired by boredom or sectarianism, presented a significant risk to public safety. The Protestant gangs, like the Billy Boys, and their Catholic equivalents took their aggression to the streets. As did the razor gangs of the East End. Enter maybe Glasgow's most famous policeman, Percy Sillitoe. A Londoner, and having already curbed the gangs of Sheffield, he was welcomed among the city councillors as the iron fist necessary. Recruiting ferocious no-nonsense officers, introducing wireless radio communications and localised forensics and fingerprint recording, he dramatically improved policing for the city. He was also a key driver in the recruitment of women into the forces that he worked in.

The death penalty did, of course, exist in Scotland for the most serious crimes, with the last execution being the hanging of Henry Burnett in 1963. More recent decades witnessed more gang-dominated years in the 1960s and plenty of individual criminals for the Glasgow authorities to bring to justice. Peter Tobin was convicted of multiple rapes and murders in the 1990s, his sentence being cut short by his death in prison in 2022. The similar crimes committed by the man chillingly known as 'Bible John' have led to speculation that the never-caught alias could even have also been Tobin.

Perhaps the lowest chapter for Glasgow's law enforcement bodies was the shambolic case of Oscar Slater, a German national wrongly convicted of the brutal murder of Marion Gilchrist in 1909. Sentenced originally to hang and then, due to public outcry, to life imprisonment, he spent the best part of twenty years in jail as a result of a prosecution case based on speculative and circumstantial evidence. Over time, the case crumbled and the likelihood of a frame-up emerged, with Slater released and financially compensated in 1929 to conclude an outrageous miscarriage of justice.

The brutal East End attack on the woman known as Carol X in 1980 was another such case. Gang raped and razor slashed repeatedly by a group of young men, her arrested attackers almost walked free after a botched Crown legal case, despite extensive evidence of guilt. Only another public outcry and the highly unusual step of presenting a private prosecution navigated the mess and saw prison convictions delivered.

As for prisons, the only one remaining in Glasgow is Barlinnie, the largest in Scotland, located in Riddrie. Hangings took place here between 1947 and 1960, though in recent times it has been used for males serving prison terms under four years. Barlinnie is expected to be closed and replaced in the coming years.

A tribute to the city's brave firefighters, which stands outside Central Station.

In 1975 the City of Glasgow Police force became part of Strathclyde Police, which in turn was consumed by a new national service, Police Scotland, in 2013. The excellent Glasgow Police Museum in Bell Street is the place to go to delve deeper.

Glasgow has long had problems with fire. The devastating blazes at the School of Art in 2014 and 2018 are the most recent poignant memories for us, but countless lives have been lost in the city over the last century to blazes. The Cheapside Street fire of 1960 and the James Watt Street fire of 1968 were large-scale killers, and Kelvin Hall had been completely destroyed by a blaze in 1925. Domestic outbreaks were very common too. The Cheapside Street disaster occurred at a whisky bonded warehouse in a blaze that escalated dramatically following explosions within as the barrels ruptured. Four hundred and fifty firemen and dozens of engines battled the blaze and it took a full week to extinguish, with nineteen of the rescuers losing their lives in the process. The James Watt Street fire saw twenty-two factory employees perish, many as a direct result of being trapped inside due to the windows being barred. Needless to say, building standards in the city needed an urgent review.

Then there was the Great Storm of 1968, which saw hurricane-force winds hit Glasgow on the 14th and 15th of January. Winds exceeding 100mph caused destruction and casualties across much of Central and Lowland Scotland, with emergency services caught unprepared as a change of course saw it sweep in unexpectedly off the Atlantic. An invisible, unshackled beast, it screamed its way up Glasgow's streets, ripping off chimneys, roofs and gable ends as it went and leaving a war zone in its wake. Around a quarter of a million homes were damaged, twenty-one people killed and hundreds more injured in what remains one of the worst natural disasters to hit a nation that has had blessedly few.

This century had also, of course, seen technological improvements within the service, with the first motorised fire engines purchased for Glasgow in 1905. The Glasgow Fire Service had been formed in 1948 but the fragmented geographic approach – with teams serving their own regions around the city – was scrapped in 1975 when the Strathclyde Fire and Rescue Service was formed as Scotland's largest brigade. In 2013 this was amalgamated into a national fire service for all of Scotland.

The modern concept of the Welfare State in the United Kingdom first came into being in the early 1900s under the Liberal Party, who instigated a series of reforms between 1906 and 1914 aimed at improving health, education and general living standards. A shocking – but fortunately short-lived – bubonic plague outbreak in Glasgow in 1900 underlined how urgently improved healthcare was required, as dire issues resulting from poor sanitation and overcrowding were underlined. The minimum wage was introduced in 1909, free school meals started in 1906 and the National Insurance Act of 1911 started the provision of free medical treatment. But it was perhaps the Beveridge Report during the Second World War that shook the system most. Given the increase in government involvement in people's lives during the war, particularly with the rationing system, there was a momentum to keep this going to help get those struggling within society to get back on their feet, and to more generally improve equality. The 1942 Report laid out a process on which today's benefit system is still based. The centralised National

Health Service for Scotland was established in 1948 with the aim of standardising healthcare across the country through nationalisation. Pay inequality was also addressed, most noticeably because women workers stepping in for men during the war were paid considerably less for doing the same job. This, coupled with improvements in education and health, meant that from the 1950s it became increasingly possible for both parents to be in full-time employment.

CONSTRUCTION AND ARCHITECTURE

To close the century, Glasgow was named the 1999 City of Architecture and Design, having already been named the 1990 European City of Culture. The latter award saw the city become the first in Britain to achieve the status and signalled all sorts of future tourism opportunities in an industry that was soon to explode. A culture-led rebrand was under way and big name visitors flocked in including the Rolling Stones, Luciano Pavarotti and Frank Sinatra. I've already mentioned the legacy bestowed upon us by Glasgow's great historic architects, and that has been wonderfully complemented by some magnificent modern structures as well, many of which provided the physical spaces for this cultural revolution. For me personally, the greatest building of them all remains the Kelvingrove Art Gallery and Museum. Its construction was made possible largely down to the proceeds from the 1888 International Exhibition, with the Museum as it looks today opened in 1901. A Spanish Baroque-style design, it is both intricate and intimidating, resplendent in red sandstone,

Kelvingrove Art Gallery and Museum.

naturally. Another exhibition inaugurated the gallery and museum, attracting 11.5 million visitors and generating income towards improving Kelvingrove Park and contributing to the establishment of the gallery's collections.

Kelvingrove was always much more than just an impressive building and it kicked Glasgow on into a new league of cultural wealth. The 1911 Scottish Exhibition of History, Art and Industry broadcast Glasgow as the cultural capital of the nation, with Kelvingrove again the setting. A series of attractions and displays were created in what was an urban theme park of its day. Palaces of history and art, a recreated Highland village, Charles Rennie Mackintosh's Cranston Tea Rooms and even an aerial railway crossing the Kelvin kept the 9 million visitors entertained throughout the summer. The gallery's biggest moment came in 1952 when the museum director, Tom Honeyman, decided to go all-in with the museum budget and purchase Salvador Dalí's 'Christ of St John of the Cross' painting. Controversial for financial and religious reasons, time has proven it to be a gamble very well taken and it still has pride of place. This despite an attempt in 1961 to damage it by a vandal. Today the dizzying museum has twenty-two galleries hosting extraordinarily diverse exhibits with everything from Renaissance art to Ancient Egypt. Rembrandt, Monet and Renoir are joined by a host of Scottish artists on display. And, crucially, it is free of charge to any with a cultural curiosity. I was frequently whisked about the place as a baby, my mum keen to shut me up no doubt, and it still has a very calming and comforting effect on me as a venue. I often find myself in there with no purpose other than to drift around, soaking up the atmosphere held within the marble and sandstone and the energy emanating from the daily organ recital, the only one in the world apparently. For all ages, it remains arguably Glaswegians' proudest possession and an absolute treasure trove for the imaginative of spirit.

Just across the road sits Kelvin Hall. Similarly presented to its better-known sibling, the building we have now was completed in 1927 – the original was made of wood and burned down – with the purpose of hosting large-scale exhibitions and events. Over the last century this has included sports, rallies, rock concerts, trade shows and even circus acts. Until moving to the Riverside in 2010 it was also the venue for the Museum of Transport, a place where my own childhood dreams soared as a youngster … and which I can somehow still smell. Very much a building dedicated to public service, it still provides sports facilities, art and cultural resources for locals.

5

TRANSPORT

THE CLYDE

The Clyde was not always the mighty force that Glaswegians of today reflect on with such pride. It was once little more than a shallow, meandering river and even the most visionary of its medieval visitors could not have begun to fathom the extent to which it would become one of the world's primary waterways. Efforts began in 1755 to artificially deepen the river as it lacked the scope for large-scale access to the Atlantic to the west. Up to this point, and during the booming tobacco trade years, landed goods were brought upriver from the likes of Greenock and Port Glasgow in smaller craft. In what must have been a laborious and thankless task, vast quantities of underwater silt were removed by dredging. Progress was slow but steady as the final inconveniently shallow few miles of the river were eventually made navigable. The Clyde Navigation Trust had been established in 1858 with the aim of formalising the effort and maximising the performance and capacity of the river as its potential became increasingly clear. It brought all the relevant stakeholders in its success together, with the shipbuilders, industrialists, merchants and city officials charged with ensuring that supply met this new flood of demand. They oversaw the creation of tolls, the building of new docks, improvements in equipment and general upkeep of the riverside community. In truth though, until the removal of Elderslie Rock in 1886 the river still lacked the width and depth to permit the largest vessels from travelling right up to the city. The rock, a volcanic brute of a thing, had to be blasted down to a depth of 28ft using innovative engineering techniques and a combination of drilling and underwater explosives. Shortly before this point, one of the worst tragedies in the river's history occurred in 1883. The SS *Daphne* had just been launched into the water at Govan for its outfitting and finishing touches when it capsized due to anchor failure. One hundred and twenty-four of the 200 workmen aboard were killed – including many teenage boys – by the sudden sinking. The lethal dangers of ship construction horrified the local population and resulted in regulation changes during similar future outfitting procedures.

Such fortunately rare setbacks aside, the successful expansion of the river took Glasgow's economy to the next level. Heavy industry such as metal manufacturing and shipbuilding could now move inland from the coastal peripheries and scores of jobs and economic activity migrated east with them. As we have seen, by the twentieth century the city had become the worldwide home of shipbuilding. No project was too ambitious, no range too far. From the 1880s to 1930s, the Anchor Line was dispatching regular liners bound for New York, and steamers for India. From the iconic ships fit for monarchs to vessels that opened up the world for everyday families for the first time, the Clyde was the great facilitator of its day. Emigration went up a notch, with a steady stream of British and Scandinavian travellers utilising this transatlantic route to begin new lives. One of the river's many huge employers, the Anchor Line opened up new offices on both sides of the ocean, with their St Vincent Street base opening in 1907.

The Clyde of today is a much quieter place. Gone are the clangs and bangs but returned are so many of the wildlife species scared off by man's dominance. Wildfowl and waders join otters, kingfishers and the armies of gulls in looking for pickings that include plentiful brown trout and even salmon. A salute too to the Glasgow Humane Society that was founded in 1790 and remains the world's oldest life-saving society, rescuing thousands of lives on Glasgow's waterways. A lifeboat service with the purpose of preserving life throughout Greater Glasgow, they still provide educational services to emergency services and members of the public on practising safety on the water.

THE CANALS AND WATERWAYS

Domestic trade opportunities for Glasgow soared with the long-awaited opening of the Forth & Clyde Canal in 1790, a move that connected the east and west of Scotland and allowed for the movement of goods to Edinburgh. The North Sea was also now in play – with no need to take the long, potentially perilous way round – and the markets of Scandinavia and mainland Europe ensured further growth.

The opening of the Carron Iron Works near Falkirk in central Scotland in 1759 had changed the landscape for iron and steel, and the movement of heavy goods on a huge scale was also now possible as a result of the canal. Ships could now slice into the industrial heart of Scotland rather than having to work their way around the often treacherous north headland or risk attack by French ships to the south, given that the Napoleonic Wars were raging at the turn of the century. With time, the canals dwindled and declined as train travel took the nation by storm and larger ships were unable to fit along the narrow sections of the network. The canal was to close in the 1960s but National Lottery funding in 2000 saw the creation of the Falkirk Wheel, an impressive boat-lifting engineering feat that allowed the connection of the Forth & Clyde Canal with the Union Canal and therefore a waterway between Glasgow and Edinburgh once again.

Glasgow-born David MacBrayne contributed to the west coast waterways immeasurably by creating the fleet that connected the city to the communities of the Highlands and islands. From the mid-nineteenth century, his shipping routes operated between the Clyde Estuary and points along the challenging geography of the west coast using the Crinan Canal to reach Oban and the Caledonian Canal to get to the Highland capital of Inverness. Caledonian MacBrayne ferries still operate numerous popular routes with their fleet exceeding thirty ferries, fulfilling the vital task of transporting locals, commercial traffic and tourists between the mainland and Hebridean islands. Since 1969, Calmac has been wholly nationalised and is heavily subsidised, despite enjoying a near-monopoly over west coast transport. It's fair to say islanders in particular enjoy a love–hate relationship with the operator these days as the ageing fleet continually leads to cancellations and delays.

GETTING ABOUT TOWN

In the times of the Tobacco Lords, the wealthy would have taxied their way about by horse or horse-drawn cart. Many would have owned their own Clydesdales, some in their own urban stables. Public transport didn't properly exist until the mid-nineteenth century but it too would have relied on horses. By the early 1870s there were several dozen horse-drawn omnibus services in operation but these were soon phased out with the arrival of the tram. Also horse-drawn initially, the first electric trams entered the city streets in 1898, requiring the ripping up of much of the town centre to install the tramlines. The formation of the Glasgow Corporation Tramways saw the council become the first local authority in Britain to run its own public transport system and by 1900 Glasgow's tram passenger numbers represented fully one-fifth of the passengers using trams in all of England and Wales. The rickety-rackety fun cars were to boss the streets for decades and, despite the safety risks and the breakdowns, they were much loved. Powered by overhead wires and running on tracks, the tram network grew rapidly and extensively to even permit journeys well outwith the city limits. During the First World War, thousands of staff signed up to fight abroad and the trams were one of the many examples where women stepped in for the first time to keep the city running. They were to last right up to the 1960s when, in 1962, a parade of the vast and varied fleet was arranged by way of a send-off. Around 250,000 are said to have attended to sadly bid farewell to this mainstay of city life. But with Edinburgh having brought them back in recent years, and the need to reduce road vehicle emissions more vital than ever, we may not have seen the last of them.

Omnibuses started arriving on the scene too, in the mid-1830s. They principally moved people back and forth to the Clyde's harbours and employment areas. Their popularity led to the need for Glasgow's first highway code. Trolleybuses were similar to the trams and overlapped with their lifespan, operating from 1949 to 1967. Also using overhead electricity lines, they were not, though, restricted by tracks and could move more flexibly, often taking passengers closer to their homes. Cheekily referred to as 'the Silent Death' by locals, their noiseless sneak-up-on-me-would-you? movement would have startled plenty of pedestrians in their brief lifespan. Used throughout Britain at the time, Glasgow had the largest investment in them outside of London with around 200 in operation, serving eight routes.

UNDERGROUND

Along with Newcastle, Glasgow is the only other city in Britain to run a subway system aside from the extensive and intimidating maze operating under London's streets. This new means of getting about was introduced to the city in 1896. A basic cable system first 'powered' the cabins, with them being hauled along between stops. Initially stopping at fifteen stations, it took around forty minutes to complete the route. Crossing the River Clyde between Partick and Govan, this was a revolutionary step forward for public transport. The offices were at St Enoch Square, in a building that has somehow held on in the face of frenetic construction surrounding it. Its architect was James Miller, one of the key minds to the designs behind Glasgow's rail systems. From the 1930s, it was all electrified at huge cost, trimming the route journey time and making it a popular and efficient option for locals.

As with anything, the network beneath the streets required maintenance and evolution, and a three-year restoration programme was undertaken in 1977. Demand had been falling post-war, vast areas of the residential areas of the city were unserved by the stops, breakdowns and delays were on the rise and industrial commutes, particularly to the shipyards, were in permanent decline. And so the system we recognise today came into being. Students from Glasgow School of Art contributed to the new carriage design, the exteriors were painted bright orange and a comprehensive rebranding was rolled out. Even the Queen made her way north for the reopening.

The subway is still very popular, particularly for shuttling passengers between the city centre and West End. Affectionately referred to as 'the Clockwork Orange' and boasting a strong retro appeal, its circular route structure is surely the most straightforward in the world. Even if you miss your stop, sit yourself back down and it'll be back around within twenty-four minutes. Why the network isn't further expanded to bring in more of the east and south of the city remains a frustration, especially given that there remain abandoned underground stops that could be reopened. I walk past a partially exposed one in the Botanic Gardens regularly, from where I peer through the fencing down at the forgotten and eerie subterranean world beneath. The mind rumbles. It remains to be seen what the next chapter holds for the system, but talk of expansion isn't going anywhere. Inexplicably, the subway cars have retained the same musty odour I remember from my 1980s childhood, despite all the renovations, replacements and countless cleans. Somehow, that's extremely comforting.

CROSSING THE CLYDE

Such a river-centred city does unsurprisingly have no shortage of crossings, with a flurry of bridges spanning between Glasgow Green in the east and the West End, crossing south. The most famous – certainly the most photographed – is the Clyde Arc, referred to in the most Glasgow way possible as the 'Squinty Bridge'. Connecting Finnieston with Pacific Quay, it serves as both a road and footbridge. Opened in 2006, it adds to the futuristic appeal of the riverside, complementing the Hydro, Riverside Museum and Glasgow Science Centre. Within a stone's throw, the pedestrian-only Bell's Bridge was added in 1988 and crosses over between the Crown Plaza Hotel on the north side and the Science Centre on the south. Originally constructed to allow convenient access to the Scottish Exhibition and Conference Centre as part of the Glasgow Garden Festival, the footbridge is built low over the waterline as few ships come this far inland, though it can

The Clyde Waterfront, where old and new collide.

be separated and pivoted to swing alongside the river banks if necessary. Its nearest neighbour to the distant west, the gigantic Erskine Bridge at Old Kilpatrick, was opened in 1971 and could more naturally accommodate the passing of large vessels beneath.

Numerous other bridges decorate the river and stretch out from the city centre. Historically, it all began over what is now Victoria Bridge, linking Bridgegate and Gorbals Street. In the thirteenth and fourteenth centuries a wooden bridge was the first crossing, before several stone upgrades gave us the five-arch bridge of today. The railway bridge crossing to the south out of Central Station is known as the Hielanman's Umbrella, presumably as it historically served as a shelter for Highlanders enduring the Glasgow climate while waiting for their train home or meeting up with fellow travellers to discuss the challenges of the day.

The striking seven-arch Glasgow Bridge (or Jamaica Street Bridge) is the second-oldest crossing point of the river, although several versions have come and gone since its beginnings in 1767. And the Kingston Bridge at Anderston encompasses the forever-busy M8 motorway. Built in the late 1960s, it ensures that Glasgow can boast the rarity of a motorway running through, rather than around, the city. Given its propensity for delays, though, drivers often turn to the Clyde Tunnel. Connecting Whiteinch and Govan, the tunnel was a necessary post-war alternative to further downstream bridges, which would only complicate the busy shipping pathways. Approved in 1948 but not actually completed until 1963, it was the first modern road crossing of the river and involved brutal conditions for the workers, 21ft under the riverbed. These included the need to adjust to the conditions in decompression chambers before and after their exhausting shifts.

Bridge building is no easy task, certainly not without the tools and expertise construction workers now have in their arsenal. Locals often opposed design ideas, and the Clyde Navigation Trust always had to give the green light too, and that's before health and safety was broached. Most have undergone repairs or rebuilds, and disasters such as that of the Tay Bridge on the east coast would never have been far from the minds of the constructing engineers. That rail bridge, in Dundee, partially collapsed in 1879 during a storm, plunging a passenger train into the water and killing all aboard. Fortunately, such a tragedy has never been seen on Glasgow's bridges.

THE RAILWAYS

Leaving arguably the most important mode of land transport to last, certainly domestically, trains were the key to opening up Glasgow to wider Britain in the Victorian years, beginning in 1837. While trains had been primarily used for industry, large-scale pleasure travel was born in the nineteenth century and wealthier Glaswegians seized the opportunity for exploration and adventure with trips out of the city. This growth would ensure a decline for the Clyde steamers and opened up rural and coastal regions previously restricted to access by sea only. By the twentieth century these changes in the transport trends of the Glaswegian were most evident at Central Station but before that, from 1840, Glasgow's main terminal had been at Bridge Street Station, south of the river. It wasn't until 1879 that trains started their comings and goings from the current site in what is now the heart of town, aside Gordon Street. Central Station also boasts its own neighbouring hotel, in itself an impressive example of Victorian architecture, but one that is often a victim of the tight grid system of the city centre that prevents a suitable vantage point from which to admire its appeal. A wonderful train station tour is available for visitors, which explores the spooky and forgotten subterranean platforms and captures its pivotal importance to the city's development.

Another competing station had been opened at St Enoch in 1876 and was overlooked by what was then the largest hotel in the city, with 200 rooms. The move across river was not a fast or straightforward one for either new station, with bridges over the Clyde and extensive building construction required. The Clyde Navigation Trust had justifiably opposed any proposals that would have hindered trade by water. But by the turn of the century, Central was a booming terminal that would soon hold thirteen southbound platforms. It received a long-awaited renovation in the 1980s and then again in the late 1990s, respecting its history and structural integrity with great sensitivity. Bridge Street Station ceased to be needed from 1905 but St Enoch Station continued until 1966. Its hotel was demolished in 1977 but the subway line still has a well-used stop on the historic site. Other smaller stations popped up all over the city as the need for goods and coal transportation accelerated, not to mention for workers' commutes.

While Central primarily catered to southbound routes, another station was required for the north, and to Edinburgh. Queen Street Station – initially called Dundas Street Station – met this need. This latest hub had been opened in 1842 but took several decades to be structurally complete. A major renovation was completed in 2021, hugely improving the visual appearance adjacent to George Square. Train services across Scotland were nationalised in 2022 after years of public complaints on the efficiency and value being provided. We like a good moan, but we do love our train travel.

THE RIVERSIDE MUSEUM

The only place to adequately experience Glasgow's transport evolution is the Riverside. Having moved around over the decades, it found its current home in 2011. Its vast and diverse collections pay tribute to a deep public interest that dates back to the 1860s when the City Industrial Museum was opened in Kelvingrove Park. Samples of engines and machinery were on display to inspire and educate at a time when Glasgow was making itself known around the world. But it was the closing down of the city's tram system in the 1960s that sparked the desire to create a collection that could be appreciated for generations to come. The old tram depot on Albert Drive was the first formal Museum of Transport, followed by an upgraded move to Kelvin Hall in 1987.

The gigantic locomotives immediately capture the visitor's attention, with the *Glen Douglas* particularly romantic as it was the train that for decades travelled the West Highland line between Glasgow and Mallaig, a route still regarded as one of the finest in Europe and made further famous by the

The Riverside Museum, stylishly designed by Zaha Hadid.

Harry Potter movies. The model ship displays are a marvel, too. The scale and detailing of the *Queen Mary*, the *QE2*, the tragic *Athenia* and many more are on display, with their intricacies a suitable testament to the extraordinary graft that went into their making. Clyde-built masterpieces indeed. It's not just the obvious that make the cut for display, with everything from personal modes of getting about such as skateboards, bicycles and gliders, to ground-breaking items like Scotland's first wheelchair-accessible taxi, a horse-drawn cabriolet for the monied in local society and, of course, a fleet of motor cars spanning the automobile's lifespan. Expect scenes ranging from *Chitty Chitty Bang Bang* to *The Italian Job* to pop into your mind's eye. Best of all, the Riverside includes a wonderfully recreated Main Street that serves as a time capsule of Glasgow from the 1890s and into the 1900s. There's a cobblers, saddlers, upholsterers, pawn brokers and an Anchor Line office that would have served as a travel agent of its day. There's even a subway stop and a bar.

For me, it will always be the Transport Museum, with Kelvin Hall its true home, and as a little boy I was never out of the place, dragging my presumably unamused parents to point at the model frigates and board the life-size buses, trams and steam engine rooms. But younger generations and today's visitors will see Zaha Hadid's impressive Riverside architectural structure as the epicentre of Glasgow's famous dynamism. Overlooking the source of countless excited launches over the centuries from the Clyde's shipyards, history hangs in the air. An evocative wander around the SS *Glenlee*, moored outside the museum, completes a very family-friendly day out.

6

DON'T GO THERE: POLITICS AND RELIGION

It's a funny old topic, one that tends to send us scurrying to the extremes of emotion. Shouting matches or stony, shackled silences are often the expected forms of communication where politics and religion are concerned and, as I've already alluded to, Glasgow has seen a more passionate relationship with the controversial pair than most. From its foundations as a burgh in 1175 when bishops and the Church ruled over the city's decision-making, to the explosive topics of Scottish independence and religious sectarianism in recent decades, you'd be forgiven for treading very lightly.

With local government having been overseen by the Church, it wasn't until 1690 that a more democratic system was firmly established. Today's Glasgow City Council has taken various names over the centuries but the running of the city has followed a similar process since. Politicians these days are elected from across Glasgow's regions to sit in both Holyrood and Westminster, with the city having traditionally sent left-leaning candidates to fill these roles. From the 1800s more formalised political parties came to the fore, with the

Liberals well supported in Scotland. Glaswegian Sir Henry Campbell-Bannerman was leader of that party, and prime minister between 1905 and 1908. Educated at Glasgow High School, he would go right to the top of British politics in a career that saw him support Irish Home Rule, oppose British 'barbarism' during the Boer War in South Africa and grant greater power to the trade unions with a view to reduced working hours. Since the Second World War, the Labour Party has relied heavily on Scottish votes as they have tussled with the right-wing Conservative Party in their duopoly for control of the British government, with Glasgow seen as one of their heartlands until the rise of the Scottish National Party in the twenty-first century.

SCOTTISH INDEPENDENCE

Throughout Scotland's history and to this day, this is the big one. The Union of 1707 brought Scotland back into a formal relationship with England following the furious efforts of William Wallace, Robert the Bruce et al. to get us out of one in the thirteenth and fourteenth centuries. But the booming economic opportunities of the British Empire, coupled with Scotland's dismal attempts to achieve something similar of its own, had triggered a new curiosity among the nation's handful of powerful decision-makers. Although the population at large was none too pleased, their views were irrelevant. Already connected through the Crown, the bond was sealed in 1707 and Scotland suddenly had the world's market on its doorstep. Vast wealth generation followed, with Glasgow's dramatic growth owing a huge amount to the faraway markets of the Empire. This assuaged most and, although never short of bumps and the odd outburst of resentment, the England–Scotland relationship continued fairly peacefully as the United Kingdom of England, Scotland, Wales and Northern Ireland remained established as one of the leading powers in the world going into the twenty-first century.

The turn of the century brought with it the culmination of decades of debate in the formation of Scotland's own Parliament. Some of the decisions affecting the nation would now be made in Edinburgh, as opposed to London, and the shiny new Scottish Parliament at Holyrood was established in 1999. With this new geographic swing came the rise in prominence of the Scottish National Party, one with the primary aim of delivering Scottish independence. They would go on to form both minority and majority governments in Edinburgh and, in 2014 with confidence rising, Scotland was asked a very big question. Should it be an independent country? It was one that gripped every household in the land as everyone resident in Scotland considered an issue that had spent several years gathering fresh momentum. The disconnect with the Westminster system, the evident natural resources that Scotland was blessed with, historical animosity, resentment over British foreign policy and nuclear programme, ties of family and friendship, the harsh realities of divorce ... it all went into a volatile melting pot as we wrestled with the biggest political question we'd ever faced. A total of 85 per cent of the nation voted in the referendum, with the decision landing in favour of remaining in the Union, with the winning campaign gathering 55 per cent of the vote. An unconvincing economic case is generally regarded to have been the downfall of the 'Yes' side – those pursuing independence – with older generations in particular opposing the break-up.

Glasgow, however, was one of the few Scottish regions that voted in the other direction. A huge celebration of independence had been planned for George Square, with the atmosphere quashed as results from across Scotland started to come in. Saltire-wearing hopefuls trudged home in despondency as Union Jacks took over the square, with inevitable aggression following. The songs of 'Flower of Scotland' were met by 'Rule Britannia' as centuries of religious and political differences threatened to boil over into violence. Sectarian chanting, Nazi salutes and antisocial behaviour rubbed salt in the wounds for those Glaswegians who had held such high hopes for a different outcome and a new, optimistic beginning. On my journey to work the following morning, I've never seen my city so flat, so resigned. In truth though, this was a country divided almost right down the middle on this massive issue, and the majority of voters would concede that there were reasonable and valid arguments being made by both sides. Fortunately, acts of physical violence had remained blessedly rare but Britain's surprise withdrawal from the European Union just two years later exacerbated the outrage and reopened old wounds. A comfortable majority of Scots had opposed this Britain-wide decision, this Brexit, but were dismissed given the weight of support for leaving emanating from voters in England and Wales. The Scottish government's renewed plans for a second referendum were repeatedly blocked by Westminster, despite a surge in support for the Scottish National Party following the 2014 referendum outcome and aftermath. Ignoring the issue has been the tactic of the British government and, with the right to hold another vote resting solely in their hands, a stalemate has occurred. At the time of writing, independence remains at the forefront of everyone's mind, but a way of legally achieving it seems distant, if not impossible.

THE HISTORICAL RELIGIOUS DIVIDES

Christianity was founded in Glasgow by St Ninian, at or near the site of Glasgow Cathedral, making it a place of religious importance since the fourth century. Going almost right back to its origins and the village, town and city that grew out from the cathedral and the tomb of St Mungo, Glasgow has had Catholicism in its waters. The Catholic church established in the sixth century by St Mungo became both a place of pilgrimage to Glasgow's father and a formalised stone cathedral, the latter starting in the twelfth century. As we've already heard, the Protestant Reformation comprehensively reset religious positions across the land, and elsewhere in Europe. Fears of corruption, strong growth of Protestantism from England and the powerful oratory skills of preachers like John Knox led to the masses turning away from the Roman Catholic Church. By the mid-sixteenth century, the Pope's authority was renounced, mass was illegalised and Mary, Queen of Scots was forced to abdicate. Yet the Reformation's wrecking ball of destruction set upon all Catholic buildings was blocked from the cathedral by locals determined to respect the past.

Protestantism would dominate in Glasgow until a Catholic revival that really only gathered momentum in the nineteenth century. Immigration, particularly from Ireland, led to the two religions competing once again, with many Glaswegians fearing the undermining of the Presbyterian values that they had come to respect. Although recent decades have seen the various churches come together with a view to combat sectarianism, the Catholic–Protestant divide continues to simmer in Scotland's most populous city.

But Glasgow is, of course, a place of diverse faiths these days and a wander through the streets will reveal the synagogues, mosques and temples to prove it. The beautiful Garnethill Synagogue was the oldest purpose-built of its type in Scotland, opening in 1879, with Glasgow proudly having

The cathedral, still the heart of historic Glasgow.

a strong Jewish community and a long history of sheltering those escaping persecution. Immigration from across Europe and Asia has brought us so much, and the large Muslim population in particular is an integral part of the city's societal fabric. Indeed, in 2023 Humza Yousaf, himself a Member of the Scottish Parliament for Glasgow, succeeded Nicola Sturgeon as First Minister of Scotland, becoming the first Muslim to hold the office. But, for visitors, Glasgow's multiculturalism is perhaps most obvious in a culinary sense. The quality of a Glasgow curry is almost unmatched, with the city offering some of the finest Indian and Pakistani restaurants in the world, to the extent that they have almost been adopted as national dishes. There may be no finer an example of magnificent culinary collision than the Haggis Pakora. And fortunately, tolerance and support of alternative faiths is extremely high, in contrast to the long-standing image of Celtic–Rangers football matches turning the city into some sort of giant bear pit.

'RED CLYDESIDE'

I've already touched on the resolute views that Glasgow has towards fairness, and how that seems central to the city's personality. Going right back to the Calton Weavers' protest in 1787 when linen industry workers were being phased out through no fault of their own to be replaced by machines, Glaswegians have never been shy to put their foot down. Some 40,000 pairs of feet converged on Glasgow Green to protest the Corn Laws in 1816. This had seen imports to

Britain hit by tariffs and trade restrictions that were seen to strongly favour domestic farmers and landowners, with city folk none too pleased at the wealth generation this afforded them. The ultimate repeal in 1846 could be seen as a victory for free trade. Shortly afterwards, the Green was again a venue of protest as 60,000 people around the city went on strike during the 'Radical War'. In the tough economic aftermath of the Napoleonic Wars, some workers had taken to carrying out military drills on the Green seemingly in preparation for an uprising. The nationwide rebellion was put down by force, with one of the leaders of the protest in Glasgow, James Wilson, hanged and beheaded in the Green in front of a crowd of around 20,000 onlookers. These protests were not entirely in vain, however. The 1832 Scottish Reform Act really kick-started the rollout of voting law change, with the disenfranchisement of all but the wealthiest in the population gradually being dismantled over the course of the following century.

The strike at the Singer sewing machine factory in Clydebank in 1911 is perhaps the most famous of them all. The American company had utilised Glasgow as an advantageous base since the mid-nineteenth century, during which time it had created the biggest factory in the country, employing several thousand workers. With further expansion inevitable, they moved to Clydebank in 1882 and witnessed an extraordinary act of worker solidarity in 1911 when their entire workforce of over 10,000 went on strike in the face of increased workload without increased pay for a dozen female cabinet polishers. It was quite the slap in the face for the world leaders in their field, with their hostility towards trade unions brought to the fore and business brought to a standstill. Responding aggressively, Singer threatened the strikers with the permanent loss of their jobs and factory relocation. Cowed, the workers returned and the ringleaders were sacked, but the grudges were held and the marker had been put down.

The working classes continued to voice their discontent at the conditions dictated to them, particularly following the First World War, and the tension reached its climax in 1919 in George Square, where police were overrun by protesters and 'Red Clydeside', as it was becoming increasingly known, threatened revolution. Glasgow had contributed hugely to the war effort, despite widespread opposition to it, yet the wages of the day could not match spiralling costs of living. Troops were coming back home not to a land fit for heroes, but one in the midst of deep economic woe and dire living conditions. Homes didn't have toilets, health and safety procedures were not even considerations, the female heroes of the Home Front were unceremoniously ditched by employers, dole queues were endless, crime and prostitution were rising and making ends meet was becoming impossible for a growing percentage.

Tensions escalated across society, trade union power and support soared and the British government became very nervous. In January 1919 protests were centred around the length of the working week, with unions pushing for a significant reduction and a spontaneous large-scale strike commenced that threatened to bring the city to a stop. With full-on revolution feared, the authorities dramatically called in the military in what became known as Black (or Bloody) Friday. The tipping point had arrived as police battled protesters in George Square. As many of the protesters were freshly returned from the horrors of war zones they were not so easily cowed, and they numbered possibly as many as 100,000. A Sheriff, literally attempting to read the Riot Act amidst the carnage, was promptly assaulted and had his script ripped from him as pandemonium ensued and makeshift missiles were launched at the authorities. The human tsunami migrated east to Glasgow Green and outbreaks occurred in other parts of the city too as the police were beaten back, with some stripped naked for added humiliation. No lives were lost immediately but countless were injured on both sides and one policeman would die as a result of his injuries in the aftermath.

Winston Churchill, Secretary of State for War at the time, finally pressed the panic button and called in the troops. They came from non-local barracks and were mainly English conscripts, with the government fearful of divided loyalties and the aggression worsening. They poured into the city's stations with barbed wire, tanks and machine guns deployed to guard George Square. Finally defeated, workers returned to their jobs and the leaders were arrested. Nationwide media, including some local papers, painted a picture of them as Bolshevik thugs. The three primary ringleaders were charged with inciting a mob of 20,000 and two were given jail sentences. All three, though, would go on to hold prominent political positions. As is so often the case, the protesters were widely regarded as justified in their outrage and even worthy of heroism to some. By way of short-term victory, when the temperature had settled, the working week was reduced from fifty-four to forty-seven hours. Glasgow's growing socialist feeling was only further cemented in the psyche of the city's inhabitants.

THE SUFFRAGETTES

The subject of voting rights consumed Britain before and after the First World War. Even in the face of victory, here was a country that had suffered immensely but that had pulled together in an extraordinary fashion for collective gain. Across society, the contributions and sacrifices made had been immense. Yet, the powers of voting and of democracy were still far from universal across British society. Women, specifically, could not vote at all, and this led to the formation of the women's activist movement, the Suffragettes. Across Britain their members engaged in acts of civil disobedience – chaining themselves to railings, disrupting events and storming Parliament. Emily Davison was killed when throwing herself in front of the king's horse at the Epsom Derby in 1913. Some of the those arrested went on hunger strike and were ordered to be force fed in scenes akin to medieval torture. The contribution on the Home Front, presumably coupled with the brave efforts of the Suffragettes, resulted in the 1918 Representation of the People Act acknowledging the need for at least some women to be enfranchised.

On the Glasgow side of this movement, Helen Crawford and Dorothea Chalmers Smith were two of the most prominent. Crawford was one of those who engaged in a hunger strike while imprisoned and was also involved in the Red Clydeside strike actions, as well as being a member of the Independent Labour Party. She branched off from the latter to run for the Communist Party in Govan in 1918, a movement that never took off despite plenty of rumblings. She did, though, co-found the Glasgow branch of the Women's International

League for Peace and Freedom (which still exists) with a purpose to unite women in standing up to oppression and exploitation. Dorothea Chalmers Smith was another of the famous hunger strikers. Born in Dennistoun and graduating from Glasgow University in 1894, she was a medical doctor with strong views on the treatment and arrest of leading Suffragette Emmeline Pankhurst. Sentenced to eight months in prison for her protest (attempted arson), her sentence was interrupted by her refusal to eat and subsequent ill-health. She was awarded a Hunger Strike Medal from the movement, which was donated to the People's Palace after her death.

In Kelvingrove Park can be found the Suffrage Oak tree, of Hungarian origin, that was planted in 1918 to mark the right of at least some women to legally vote from this point onwards. An audience (mainly of women) gathered to mark the historic moment that was seen as a great and just victory for the many suffrage organisations that had campaigned so vocally to have voting equality respected. Despite some bruising run-ins with storms, it still stands tall in the park over a hundred years later.

Further Rumblings in the Twentieth Century

The Billy Boys of Bridgeton were the largest of the numerous gangs operating in Glasgow during the 1920s and '30s. Named after King William of Orange, they were the Protestant-supporting group that regularly clashed with their Catholic-supporting adversaries, including the Norman Conks and Calton Tongs. The Irish immigration to Glasgow may have been behind the breaking factions in society, with resentment and limited work fuelling the fire. The Billy Boys leader, Billy Fullerton, was a member of the British Fascists political party and they aligned too with Oswald Mosley's supporters from across wider Britain. Mosley was the former senior Member of Parliament who was leading fascism at British political levels at the time. The Loyal Orange Institution, or Orange Order, carried on some of their traditions in the aftermath of policeman Percy Sillitoe's dismantling of the gangs and still stand vocally in support of British Unionism, most notably in Ireland and on the topic of Scottish independence. The 'Billy Boys' song is one synonymous with sectarianism and has been banned from Scottish football grounds but is still heard sung at matches to this day. Organised Orange Walks, meanwhile, still occur regularly in Glasgow and involve controversial marches through the city with participants kitted out in traditional regalia and musical accompaniment. Although seen as potentially volatile and strongly disliked by many local residents, the marches are policed and instances of physical violence are rare.

I have mentioned the Great Storm of 1968 already and it is a fine example of why Scots, and I think Glaswegians most specifically, still feel a great disconnect from the centre of British politics in the south. For the hurricane caused massive damage to Glasgow, with a death toll in the dozens, a massive list of casualties and an infrastructure and housing disaster on a scale not seen since the Blitz. Yet, support from the government in London was dismally stingy. A mere £500,000 loan was offered, an amount that would not cover more than a tiny fraction of the damage. Just as gallingly, the media interest in the catastrophe disappeared quickly and the level of compassionate support and sympathy went with it. The view, held by many, is of a very blatant centralised mindset of those in power in southern England. Wealth, opportunity, funding, cultural understandings ... they do not flow north as fairly as they should. These days, the corrective action being undertaken is referred to as 'levelling up' – the notion of decentralising power to the at-times-forgotten regions of the United Kingdom. A finer euphemism you may never hear. But there can be no doubt that resentment and support for Scottish independence owes much to the perception of this long-term slight.

The chapter has to close with Margaret Thatcher. Ask anyone of a certain generation in Glasgow about the Iron Lady and you are unlikely to receive a passive response. The rush to privatisation and, most controversially, the Poll Tax overseen by the British Prime Minister (serving between 1979 and 1990) saw a change to the taxing abilities of local councils that ultimately resulted in greater taxation for poorer households. This policy, central to Thatcherism, was introduced in Scotland a year before being rolled into England and Wales, a gesture that has led to the commonly held view that Thatcher saw Scotland as something of a guinea pig. In any case, there was a furore as masses simply refused to pay and civil unrest followed. Although the deeply unpopular policy was quickly scrapped under her successor, John Major, Thatcher's legacy continues to hinder the Conservative Party in Scotland even still. The North remembers, as George R.R. Martin might put it.

7

THE WAR YEARS

I have already touched on the conflicts that have historically consumed Glasgow. I've explored the minimal presence of the Romans around Glasgow, the absence of any significant medieval tussling and how the two world wars impacted massively on Glasgow's industry and economy in the twentieth century; how the latter presenting huge manufacturing opportunities and demand, with an unprecedented need for ships, motorised vehicles and heavy machinery. But also how both wars were followed by dramatic slumps as economic depression gripped the nation. And it's these epic conflicts that require a deeper dive. The politics, the physical and emotional impact, the social and economic fallout … in we go.

FIRST WORLD WAR (1914–18)

The Great War was, of course, a war of alliances. Britain joined with the Allies principally comprising France, the United States, Japan, Russia and Italy against the Central Powers of Germany, Austria–Hungary and the Ottoman Empire. Famously starting with the assassination of the heir presumptive to the throne of Austria–Hungary, Archduke Franz Ferdinand, the existing alliance system between nations triggered a shocking escalation into a conflict on a geographic scale never before imagined. It saw the death of an estimated 9 million soldiers and over 5 million civilians across the planet. In Europe, it was a war of trenches, of attrition, and of ever-increasing pointlessness. Soldiers on battlefronts sheltered in the mud for years as guns, grenades, tanks and even poison gas were utilised in attempts to break a grim stalemate over territory. A mid-war revolution in Russia allowed the Central Powers to focus their energy on the Western Front but the arrival of the United States into the conflict in 1917 tipped the balance in favour of the Allies and forced the abdication of Germany's Kaiser Wilhelm II in November 1918, and the end of the war.

Glasgow, meanwhile, largely observed the war from a safe distance and the city itself was fortunate not to be subjected to direct attack. What cannot be contested, though, is the huge contribution made by the city to the war effort. In terms of sacrifice, around 200,000 men (around a fifth of its population) enlisted, with close to 20,000 losing their lives. Initially, joining was based on volunteering, with an early enthusiasm to enlist soon tempered with the realisation and mounting dread that this conflict would not be concluded quickly. Incentives to counter this included the creation of 'Pals Battalions', whereby friends, families, neighbourhoods and communities were assured to be placed together in the far-off lands where they had been sent to risk everything. This made it less intimidating perhaps for the men being conscripted, but the result was, of course, emotionally devastating for those left behind if whole families or groups were killed at the same time. From Glasgow, those departing included the 15th, 16th and 17th Highland Light Infantry Battalions. A particularly impressive Glasgow-born artist, Muirhead Bone, joined them, having been enlisted by the War Propaganda Bureau to be the first official war artist. His sketches of war-torn France were hoped to inspire the patriot within more young men. But with enthusiasm dwindling rapidly as news spread of the dire conditions in the trenches, conscription was implemented with the passing in January 1916 of the Military Service Act, with almost all single men between the ages of 18 and 41 compulsorily required to fight.

The tumult was certainly not restricted to the war zones, however, as the evidence from the Home Front will testify. As we've seen in previous chapters, it fell largely to women to step on to factory floors to replace the departed men and keep the city's vital industries running. In 1911, fewer than 6,000 women were employed on Clydeside, while by 1918 more than 31,000 were working in munitions alone – roughly one in three women were employed in their roles as substitutes for men. Not just that, either, as medical pioneers such as Glasgow University graduate and Victoria Infirmary surgeon Anne Louise McIlroy pitched in on the front lines on the Continent. Leading a Scottish Women's Hospital unit in France and Greece, she would also join the Royal Army Medical Corps. It was these vital contributions that – at least in part – led to women finally being granted the right to vote in 1918. Gender equality in voting in Britain was not, however, achieved until 1928. Education suffered too, with Glasgow University facing a staffing crisis and the necessity to offer up lecture rooms for military training exercises and recruitment drives. Naturally the birth and marriage rates declined during the war years, but there was a dramatic 'baby boom' at the cessation of hostilities with record-breaking 1920 seeing more than 137,000 births registered in Scotland. Folk had to celebrate somehow.

Militarily, Glasgow provided, in the form of munitions and weaponry, a potentially outcome-changing amount to the British cause. The National Projectiles Factory was operated by William Beardmore & Co. in Cardonald and the pressure on workers in these factories to maintain consistently high output of armaments and equipment would have been intense. And, of course, there was the provision of ships, land vehicles and aircraft, all overseen by the Clyde and its workers.

There had been an arms race dating back to the 1870s and the unification of Germany, with a newly emboldened German leadership keen to compete with Britain's superior navy in particular. Known as the 'dreadnought' shipbuilding race, thanks to Britain and Germany's competition to create the most dreadnought battleships between 1909 and 1914, this too helped to escalate tensions between the countries even before the war formally commenced. Glasgow's might in shipbuilding, steel and engineering was focussed almost exclusively on the war effort with RMS *Aquitania*, *Lusitania*, *Caledonia* and *Waverley* just some of the Clyde-built giants to pitch in during the war. Some of the Anchor Line's vessels had been chartered during the Boer War in South Africa in 1899 but were fully requisitioned in the First World War, with some being transformed into auxiliary warships and facing potential enemy attack from above and below the waterline.

Several of the line's ships were torpedoed between 1916 and 1918, with seven lost. Convoys became normal as a result of devastating attacks on merchant shipping in the North Atlantic, with safety in numbers serving as both a deterrent and to ensure vastly improved rescue prospects for any ships in peril. It's an extraordinary thing to reflect on – a whole city, and indeed country, working in a unified effort with a sole overriding aim and purpose. The war was everything.

With no construction going on during the war, soldiers returned to a city that was struggling badly. Immediate unemployment was common among those expecting a heroic homecoming. Those looking to enter education joined a flood of demand that the universities couldn't cope with and it would be several years before student recruitment levels became manageable. Unfortunately the war economy didn't just cease overnight; the process of demobilisation would drag on. Industrial action was inevitable. As we've seen, 'Black Friday' of 1919 was one of the worst riots in Glasgow's history. Things would go from bad to worse in the fallout from war as the difficult economic conditions already discussed in the 1930s resulted in damaging social issues and the creation of slum neighbourhoods in various parts of the city.

Today the Cenotaph memorial in George Square commemorates those who gave their lives in the conflicts of the twentieth century, though it was originally for those who perished in the First World War. To this day, crowds still congregate here to mark moments of reflection for all who were lost. The memorial was unveiled in 1924 by Field Marshal Earl Haig with the inscription 'Their name liveth evermore'.

SECOND WORLD WAR

The fallout from the First World War gripped Europe, with Germany heavily punished by the terms of the Treaty of Versailles and given a steep bill of reparations that its economy struggled hopelessly to deliver. Faced with hyper-inflation and severe economic depression, Germany was one of numerous nations that embraced the rise of fascism. A certain Adolf Hitler was at the forefront of this movement, a deliverer of furiously passionate speeches that promised reward in return for aggressive action, specifically in the form of pursuing a foreign policy centred around territorial expansion. In 1934, he became the Führer, Germany's head of state, and in September 1939 his invasion of Poland triggered a declaration of war from Britain and France. This time the wartime alliances would go on to be principally made up of the Allies including Britain, France, the Soviet Union and the United States, who united against the Axis powers of Germany, Italy and Japan. New technologies dictated that this war would now also be fought largely from the air and under the water with the threat of weapons of mass destruction replacing the slow-moving, tit-for-tat reality of trench warfare. Easily the most devastating conflict the world has ever seen, there were somewhere between 70 and 85 million fatalities. It was a war that saw genocides including the Holocaust, large-scale bombing across the globe, the Battle of the Atlantic for control of the seas, the deadly Normandy beach landings and the Battle of Britain to defend the island from Luftwaffe fighters in the skies above. Bravery and endurance stood up to evil and pain on a scale the planet had never seen until the Nazis were gradually defeated, Germany invaded and Japan finally forced into surrender in 1945.

While the First World War may have had a slightly detached and distant feel, given Scotland's geographic protection from the land fighting, this new conflict was immediately something different. With the declaration of war ringing in the ears of British citizens, a degree of panic consumed many in society. A desire to flee would have been entirely normal, and the Glasgow-built *Athenia* was one of many ships hastily set for the long journey across the Atlantic. The relative safety of North America must have seemed extremely appealing, not least for the many Canadians and Americans who squeezed tightly on board anxious to get as far away from what was gearing up to be a primarily European conflict as quickly as possible. Little did they know they would be the victims of what is thought to have been the first shot fired at sea in the Second World War as, having departed Glasgow and off the coast of Ireland, the *Athenia* fell victim to a German U-boat torpedo. While most of the passengers were saved by the ship's lifeboats and nearby rescue ships, 112 people died. It was a stark warning of the horrors to come.

As war approached, ships were once again requisitioned en masse by the Admiralty. While the transatlantic ferries adopted grim new purposes, the *Cameronia* was for a time the only option for those trying to exit Europe. It carried large numbers of children and other evacuees, including Jews fleeing Germany. Its commander, David Bone, noted in his memoirs that carrying 400 children across the Atlantic alone, without the security of a convoy, was 'the most wearing and anxious of all my days at sea'. The thought of that responsibility, in such vast isolation, without even the luxury of being able to put the ship's lights on at night, and with the omnipresent lurking danger of the silent submarines, is chilling. Zig-zagging evasively, the ship successfully reached New York. But plenty of others were not so successful and screams of 'Abandon Ship!' would no doubt have haunted the dreams of all seamen of the time. In one astonishing tale, the Anchor Line's *Britannia* was sunk off the coast of Africa in 1941 with survivors clambering aboard lifeboats amidst the chaos. One of these found itself holding eighty-two people, despite only being built for fifty-six. Conditions made landing in Africa impossible and the small craft actually took on the length of the Atlantic to somehow arrive in Brazil some twenty-three days later. Over half of those aboard the ship lost their lives in the attack but thirty-eight of those on that remarkable lifeboat survived.

Perhaps the most fearsome chapter in the war from a domestic perspective was the infamous Blitz. Occurring over 1940 and 1941, this saw a mass aerial bombardment of Britain by the Luftwaffe. Although the Germans had lost the Battle of Britain for air superiority – an event that overlapped with the Blitz – the Luftwaffe still had the capability to inflict damage on the ground and did so most savagely to London for a staggeringly relentless fifty-six days and nights. Industrial and urban areas across Britain were targeted, with Clydebank largely destroyed in March 1941. With its shipyards and manufacturing facilities the target, 1,650 incendiary containers and 272 tonnes of bombs rained down on the town and indiscriminately caused chaos and death among the civilian population. Although less than 10 miles to the east, Glasgow itself managed to avoid the vast majority of the carnage in what was the worst incident to occur in Scotland during the war. The main memorial to the atrocity is to be found at the Dalnottar Cemetery. Among the reasons that the damage to the city and the wider area was not even worse was the use of decoys, a tactic to exacerbate the confusion of night bombings for enemy pilots. In Glasgow's case, a 'Starfish' decoy site was set up near the Campsie Fells, a sparsely populated rural area to the north. A decoy village was also built on the Isle of Bute. Anything combustible was collected along with equipment to replicate the effect of a city aflame. It is thought that around 100 bombs were dropped in the hills surrounding the city, with the decoy tactics potentially saving countless lives.

With sacrifices being made by all across the board, rationing was one of the most challenging for those at home. The German U-boats caused havoc to supply lines and the importing of foodstuffs became increasingly perilous, not to mention the destruction caused by bombing to factories on the British mainland itself. In Glasgow, and wider Britain throughout the war, citizens would queue up with their ration books to receive their allocation of staples like cheese, sugar and meat. Receiving tins of powdered milk and eggs became the norm. And, God forbid, sweetie rationing was even introduced in 1942! There had been degrees of rationing during the First World War in Glasgow too, but this was of another level in the quest to feed hungry mouths. Stockpiling also became an issue – less in the personal hoarding of toilet rolls that we've seen in more recent supply crises and more from suppliers who held back stock to stagger their profits or even hike prices as desperation escalated. It would be into the

1950s before international trade was fully operational once again, and 1954 before rationing was ended.

Glasgow's fire services had been largely separated into the city's regions and suburbs but the risk of bombing led to a greater need for co-ordinated strategy. The Auxiliary Fire Service was set up and included the recruitment of women firefighters for the first time. Although limited in number, there were several bombs that did land in Glasgow itself. Numerous tenement housing blocks were destroyed in Hyndland, Partick, Tradeston and others, resulting in several hundred victims and enormous strain and trauma for emergency service workers. In schools, children rehearsed procedures for attack and got familiar with wearing gas masks. Over 100,000 children and vulnerable people had been hastily evacuated from the city at the initial outbreak of war, with many sent to facilities or private homes in the Highlands or Ayrshire. Known nationwide as Operation Pied Piper, the amount of time they remained away from home varied significantly. A voluntary arrangement, some parents chose for their children to stay at home and face the risks together as families and communities. For those who left, they were generally separated from their family with the children recording experiences ranging from fun adventures to heart-breaking homesickness and even abuse at the hands of their host families.

Glasgow had its own Royal Air Force Auxiliary squadron of volunteers, 602 (City of Glasgow) Squadron, who were charged with protecting the skies over the city and wider area. The squadron may have been responsible for downing the first German aircraft of the war in 1939, while protecting a convoy making its way to the River Forth. I say *may* because

603 Squadron out of Edinburgh made the same claim as it was a joint effort, but obviously Glaswegians have only been calling it debatable out of politeness. The pilots were awarded the Distinguished Flying Cross for their acts, the first of many. The squadron also contributed heroically in the Battle of Britain in the skies over southern England, downing a further eighty-nine planes. With momentum swinging towards the Allies, 602 Squadron took their aircraft into attack mode over the Continent in the war's later years and are credited by the RAF for taking out the car carrying the German army commander, Field Marshal Erwin Rommel, in Normandy and ending his involvement in the war through injury.

A couple of special mentions are due. The first goes to Sergeant Gunner John Hannah, from Scotstoun, who became Scotland's first recipient of the Victoria Cross, the military's highest honour. Part of an RAF crew assigned to bomb German installations in Belgium, his plane came under heavy attack from anti-aircraft guns and sustained massive damage. All but two of the crew parachuted out with the plane shot full of holes and on fire, but 18-year-old Hannah set about furiously bringing the blaze under control to the extent that the battered plane could somehow continue its journey back to Britain. His old school in Scotstoun still gives out the John Hannah Trophy each year to their most distinguished pupil. The second goes to 'Gentle' Johnny Ramensky, a career criminal who was recruited into the military and trained in explosives. Behind enemy lines he would James Bond his way into stealing enemy documents and blowing safes, including supposedly one belonging to the Luftwaffe commander, Hermann Goering. Despite spending a large chunk of his life in (and repeatedly escaping) prisons, he was famously affable and was given the Military Medal for his exploits.

Amidst all the horror, tragedy and sacrifice, something truly bizarre happened around 10 miles south of Glasgow in 1941. Rudolph Hess, Hitler's deputy Führer and long-time ally in the Nazi command structure, was on a one-man flight that crashed at Eaglesham, with Hess jumping out using his parachute and being citizen-arrested by an excited local farmer. After a cup of tea in the farmer's cottage, Hess demanded to speak with the Duke of Hamilton, who lived nearby. By now under a more formal arrest and in the Maryhill Barracks in Glasgow, he then informed a presumably flabbergasted Hamilton that he had come to broker a peace deal between Britain and

Cameronians War Memorial outside Kelvingrove Art Gallery and Museum.

Germany. All sorts of theories – some of the conspiratorial variety – have been floated as to why Hess flew solo from Germany to land in a field in Scotland to speak with a man who on the face of it had absolutely no idea why the Nazi high command would regard him as an ally in the engineering of a peace deal. The presumption seems to be that Hess was desperate and was seeing an opportunity where there wasn't one, flying to Scotland on his own initiative. In any case, he remained under arrest, was declared mentally unstable by the doctors who examined him at Buchanan Castle in Drymen and was then transferred to the Tower of London to begin his long imprisonment. Meanwhile, back in Germany, Hitler declared his former friend insane and permanently disowned him, ordering that he be shot on sight if ever seen again in Germany. In the post-war Nuremburg Trial, Hess was sentenced to life imprisonment, which he served in Berlin.

8

CITY LIFE AND EDUCATION

For a nation that takes education so seriously, it's been a bumpy ride to the modern-day universal opportunities for learning. As with everything in the early days of Glasgow's story, the Church, overseen firstly by St Mungo and then his legacy, was interwoven deeply and provided the beginnings of an educational service. The Choir School of Glasgow Cathedral, founded in 1124 and controlled by the Church until 1872, is thought to be the oldest school in Scotland and would blossom into Glasgow Grammar School and then today's private High School of Glasgow. Latin and Greek grammar were at the heart of those earliest teachings, with James IV ordering members of the Scottish legal system to commit to learning. Children of the well-to-do would start their education from around age 8 as the fabric of a lawful and structured society began to take shape.

The at times brutal Scottish Reformation of the mid-sixteenth century was another key turning point as parish schools replaced choir schools and Protestantism took hold. Government funding helped support the Kirk in providing education, with parents and other private benefactors often contributing to costs, too. Allan Glen's became the first technical school in Scotland in 1853, named after a wright who left £21,000 in his estate to create a school for boys of families from industrial backgrounds. Textile merchant David Stow founded several teaching establishments for impoverished children, starting in 1816 with a Sunday school in the Saltmarket before even going on to create a teacher training facility twenty years later. Among other pioneering practices, he pushed for the abolition of corporal punishment and the use of school playgrounds for children. These are just a couple of examples, as places of learning began to pop up at great speed as the city's economy and prospects soared. Indeed, by the early 1820s, there were 144 schools in the Glasgow area with over 16,000 pupils enrolled (about two-thirds were fee-paying). Education was still a voluntary thing, however, up until the Education (Scotland) Act of 1872. Children aged 5 to 13 were then subject to compulsory education and this would rise gradually to age 16 by 1973. Catholic and Episcopalian schools were also brought into state funding by the 1918 Act of the same name.

From 1962, 'Highers' became the primary currency for entry into university, and remain so today. The more Highers a school student gathered, in theory, the better prospects they had in their university and college applications, or in appealing directly to potential employers if they were keen to quickly enter the world of work. Entry requirements to higher education providers and the qualification structure in schools remain different between Scotland and the rest of the United Kingdom and education is devolved to the Scottish

One of Glasgow's favourite schools is now a museum, the Charles
Rennie Mackintosh masterpiece on Scotland Street.

Parliament, with key decisions made in Edinburgh and not
London. 'Selective' schooling – whereby schools could be
selective in the children they taught – was phased out by the
1970s in favour of comprehensive schooling, a move that
helped to level the playing field for children regardless of
families' financial means. Although private, fee-based schools
still exist, a standardised curriculum forms the backbone of
education in Glasgow, with only a small handful of specialist
schools available.

CLUBS AND SOCIETIES

Not all education happened in the classroom, of course,
and youngsters across Scotland have long benefitted from

membership of the numerous clubs and societies centred around early development and the learning of practical skills. The Boys' Brigade was founded in Glasgow in 1883 by William Alexander Smith, a military officer keen to instil some discipline among his Sunday school pupils. His small band engaged in recreational activities and training in the survival skills needed in the outdoors, formed around Christian values. Their first camp took place at Tighnabruaich on the west coast in 1886. The Boys' Brigade would soon go on to have gathered a worldwide following and set the standard that so many youth organisations have since followed. As of 2018, membership stands at around 750,000, with a presence in sixty countries. Boys and young men from ages 4 to 18 can join.

Competition came in the form of the Boy Scouts (I was one of them), which was born in 1908 and the Girl Scouts in the same year. The Glasgow wing of the latter was created by Allison Cargill but activities for girls were pushed towards the domestic, in line with the cringeworthy gender roles of the time. As with the Boys' Brigade, though, the Scout movement for males was geared towards sports, camping, woodcraft and backpacking.

THE UNIVERSITIES

Today Glasgow, and indeed wider Scotland, is very proud of its further education establishments. We love that we can boast some of the oldest and most prestigious universities in the world, just as we are proud that eligible Scottish students can attend them for free. International students and teachers bring in welcome funds and skills and help form a vital arm of our economy and society. This pride began with a pioneering mindset, one that took great satisfaction in spreading success. Although languages and philosophy dominated in the early times, in Glasgow's case, its true offering to future generations was industrial expertise. Navigating the needs and challenges of the war years in particular, it is a testament to their importance that so many further education providers have not only survived but have grown so impressively in the last century.

As has been touched on already, Glasgow University was the start of it all when it was founded within the cathedral, before ultimately migrating to Gilmorehill in the West End in 1870. Its own teaching hospital, the Western Infirmary, was opened shortly afterwards. The Union, such an integral part of the student experience of course, began in 1885, although shamefully it was not until 1980 that women could be admitted as members. It would go on to become a university with a very broad offering and it has delivered faculties in law, the arts, business, medicine and the social sciences. Engineering and science too, although technical education really came into being with what is now Strathclyde University.

Professor John Anderson, a teacher at Glasgow University, founded the Andersonian Institute in 1796 – through bequeathment of his property – in the hope that the study of science and natural philosophy would provide practical skills for those seeking careers in industry. Certainly not a fan of apathetic and transactional learning, he provided evening classes to complement the routines of working men, with his institute also the first of its type to offer classes to women on the same terms as men. Practical skills were now available to everyday folks on a hitherto unseen level. One of its teachers, George Birkbeck, would go on to found the Mechanics' Institute in London, taking many of Anderson's early concepts and visions worldwide. The Andersonian Institute expanded, merged, broadened its faculties and departments and changed names many times. It would finally become the University of Strathclyde in 1964 following the award of a royal charter, Britain's first technological university, and I myself studied there in its business school. It still holds dear its motto 'the Place of Useful Learning'.

Then there's Glasgow Caledonian University, which interestingly owes its existence largely to domestic science. Its origins go back to 1875 and the Glasgow School of Cookery, which would merge with the West End School of Cookery to form the Glasgow and West of Scotland College of Domestic Science, a college centred around the training of cooking, housekeeping skills and needlework, and very much aimed at women. By the 1960s men were included as the Queen's College (as it became) expanded to include medical-related courses such as physiotherapy, occupational therapy and radiography. In 1993 a merger of the Queen's College and the Glasgow Polytechnic gave us the university of today, with a broadened prospectus and a campus in the heart of the city centre beside Buchanan Street Bus Station.

HEALTHCARE AND MEDICINE

Once again, and as with just about everything else in the fledgling society, initial healthcare in Glasgow owed it all to the Church. Provand's Lordship aside, the cathedral was among the first 'hospitals', certainly the only remaining part of one. Andrew de Durisdere, Bishop of Glasgow, had founded a previous medical resting place of sorts, before St Nicholas's Hospital was built in 1471 by Andrew Muirhead, a subsequent bishop, with Provand's Lordship attached to that in some capacity.

Leprosy would have been among the grim mystery ailments assessed at St Nicholas's, before colonies were established to isolate the sick. 'The Lands of the Gorbals' were Glasgow's versions and saw the afflicted sent south of the Clyde to Brigend as the incurable and contagious disease doubtless caused hysteria and panic among communities. Plagues caused even more alarm as medieval outbreaks spread rapidly with lethal and gruesome consequences. We've touched on the outbreak of bubonic plague in 1900, but when medical care was still in its infancy little could be done, and the suffering among the densely packed dwellers can only have been horrific.

The opening of the Town's Hospital in 1731 formalised the need for medical learning but would have had to provide very general care to all in need of aid. Known as a poorhouse rather than a hospital, it provided care primarily for the elderly, young children and the mentally ill, existing until the mid-nineteenth century and overseen by the Lord Provost.

Amidst these explorative times, pioneering Joseph Black discovered oxygen, nitrogen, hydrogen and carbon dioxide, and was a student of chemistry at the university, going on to become a professor there. His discovery of latent heat in the mid-eighteenth century was a key element in the work of his friend James Watt, who we'll be taking a closer look at shortly.

The Royal Infirmary, opened in 1794, was then a critical moment in the city's medical journey. With eight wards spread over five floors, it would expand gradually over the centuries and still operates today with a capacity of around a thousand beds. More pioneering work has been done there, including that of Joseph Lister, a professor of surgery there from 1860. Alarmed that sepsis was causing the death of so many patients, his use of carbolic acid to clean surgical equipment and reduce post-surgical infections has led to him being known as the 'father of modern surgery'.

Another key arrival was Glasgow University's Western Infirmary. By 1911 – at a time when tuberculosis was soaring and infant mortality was ensuring that one in seven children born in Glasgow did not live to see their first birthdays – there were over 600 beds in the teaching hospital there, with the Infirmary continuing until 2015. One of an army of impressive medical alumni, Glaswegian Ronald David Laing graduated from the university in 1951, going on to practise psychiatry and provide an enlightened and more sympathetic approach to mental health problems, approaches that his field has embraced ever since.

Gartnavel General Hospital, on Great Western Road between Hyndland and Anniesland, was a 1973 extension to

Gartnavel Royal Hospital, which was itself a mental health facility. It now includes the Beatson, a specialist centre that provides cancer treatment to residents from across the west of Scotland. The Southern General also had voluntary origins, founded in the 1850s and located in Linthouse in the south-west. It went through significant expansions in 1872 and 1905, also closing in 2015. The formation of the NHS in 1948 brought it together with medical facilities across Britain to provide a greater standardisation of care. Until its formation, charitable healthcare was being provided on a voluntary basis at these hospitals and others around the country, and were funded by donations and generous philanthropists.

With several of Glasgow's hospitals recently closing at the same time to merge services into a single entity, the Queen Elizabeth University Hospital was born in 2015. With close to 1,700 beds and on the site of the former Southern General in Govan, it was Scotland's largest publicly funded NHS construction project. Always keen to dispense with formal naming procedures at the expense of a chuckle, it became known locally as the 'Death Star', given its futuristic, star-shaped design.

The Media

Published for the first time in 1783, *The Herald* ranks as the oldest English-speaking national newspaper in the world. In its infancy, it brought news of the end of the American War of Independence, with many of its readers doubtless taking a vested interest in developments. Then called the *Advertiser*, it was initially a weekly read for the educated and monied classes of Glasgow, becoming a daily in 1858. It has changed hands many times over the years – largely competing with Edinburgh's *The Scotsman* for broadsheet top billing – and along with its sister papers the *Evening Times* and the *Herald on Sunday* is now owned by Newsquest. Having been predictably aimed at the political right of centre while fighting to establish itself, it took on more of an anti-Establishment, anti-Union tone when owned by George Outram & Co. between 1836 and 1964. Since then it has officially been politically neutral, aside from controversially backing the 'No' vote in the 2014 referendum on Scottish independence. That position triggered complaints of a biased media landscape and angry demand for Scotland to have a leading media source that favoured independence, and so was born *The National* in 2014. The first daily newspaper in the nation to support the cause, its initial popularity predictably waned somewhat, yet it remains another complementary sister paper of *The Herald*.

The extremely popular *Daily Record* is a national tabloid with its base in the city. First published in 1895, it was (among other things) the first European daily newspaper to be printed in full colour in 1971. These days it focusses more on its digital offering. The *Glasgow Times* (*Evening Times* until 2019) is the last remaining of the 'evening' papers. It has outlasted the *Evening Citizen* which had run from 1864 to 1974 and the *Evening News*, from 1915 to 1957. The former was known for providing the Sunday service listings and was therefore the popular choice for churchgoers, while the latter was right-leaning and a reliable source for the football scores. The surviving *Glasgow Times* took pride in having an ear to the ground on local goings-on within the community. It's still available in old-fashioned vendor stalls dotted around the city centre.

9

THE GLASWEGIANS

It seems entirely appropriate that there be a chapter in this book reserved for Glasgow's finest export, its people. These are the folks who capture what Glasgow really is. The hardworking, industrious types for sure, but also the big personalities who have spread the cheek, the creativity and the grit of this city to the countless shores on which they've had an impact. I'm not going to get into the debate over whether or not you could call yourself Glaswegian if you were born there, lived there and all of that. For me, all of the below are immediately associated with and strongly represent the city, even though the amount of their lives spent in the city has varied between each of them. Most have come up already in this book but here's a closer look at those who really rose to the top. For the many omissions who also deserved a mention here, I can only apologise.

JAMES WATT (1736–1819)

I suppose with how much time we spend in front of the television we could be more grateful to the inventive work of

John Logie Baird, but the scale of Watt's contribution to the evolution of transport, heavy industry and energy just can't be overstated. He was a pioneer who changed the way the world worked.

Born in Greenock on the west coast, he moved to Glasgow in 1754 to work as an instrument maker within the university, where he was permitted to set up a small workshop and there he made and repaired barometers, telescope parts, scales and the like. Of a scientific and mathematical mind from a young age, his expertise and talents accelerated quickly. Although he did not invent the steam engine in the most simplistic sense, he dramatically improved its efficiency through the use of adding a separate condenser. Otherwise lost condensation could be made use of in a container that was separate from the cylinder but connected to it. His poking and prodding – and presumably exhaustive experimentations with heat and steam – in the mid-1760s made him aware of how wasteful the existing Newcomen model was, and thanks to his alterations it was the steam engine that ultimately powered the Industrial Revolution, when the mills were popping up all over the place. Watt was also the first to use the now commonly heard term 'horse power' as part of the sales pitch for the new engines. As they would often be replacing the work of horses, he established a measurement for the output that horses could achieve through their physical power, and compared that unfavourably with his engine, using his newly established unit of measurement. The 'watt', another electrical unit of measurement, is named in his honour. Aside from his steam engine, he also invented the smokeless furnace, steam jacket and air pump. He was also a land surveyor and contributed to the planning of the game-changing Forth & Clyde canal that connected Glasgow and Edinburgh. And he even contributed to the dredging of the shipping channels in both rivers to permit vastly improved access as sea travel began to rapidly gather pace.

Much more than an inventor, his chemical expertise and philosophical mind led to him being well liked and regarded by his peers and students. Never particularly savvy with his talents in terms of making money and doing deals, he was a great relationship-builder with a constantly explorative mind, the product of which was realised near and far. In 1819, his marine engineer son, also James, personally fitted his father's engine into the *Caledonia* and the first British steam ship was launched.

A bronze statue of Watt guards the south-west corner of George Square, erected in 1832. There is also a commemorative plaque in Glasgow Green that is said to mark the spot where Watt had his eureka moment for a separate condenser to improve the steam engine performance. Where would we be without him?

WILLIAM THOMSON, 1ST BARON KELVIN (1824–1907)

A mathematician and engineer, Lord Kelvin served as Professor of Natural Philosophy at Glasgow University for an extraordinary fifty-three years. Thomson famously calculated that –273° centigrade is the lowest possible temperature in the Universe, known as absolute zero, and is the temperature at which even the tiniest particles freeze. This formed the basis of the adopted Kelvin scale for measuring temperature. Although born in Belfast, his father's work first took him to Glasgow in 1833, where he enrolled at the university at the tender age of 10. He would then go to Cambridge to continue his education before returning north in 1846 to take up his long-held role at Glasgow University.

A pioneer in the fields of electromagnetism and thermodynamics, Thomson was also a notable inventor and financial investor. Working collaboratively with numerous peers, his groundbreaking work earned him many accolades and honorary degrees. He oversaw the implementation of the first transatlantic cable, invented the siphon recorder and patented a telegraph receiver known as a mirror galvanometer. These contributed to submarine exploration, facilitated the sending of wireless telegrams and made Thomson a great deal of money, as well as a knighthood. It's also thought that he created the first physics laboratory in Britain, while working in Glasgow. Indeed, his house in the city was among the first in the world to have been lit entirely by electricity.

Becoming a lord in 1892, he took the name 'Kelvin of Largs' in a nod to his Glasgow connection and to his home in the seaside town. While Kelvin is buried in Westminster Abbey, aside Isaac Newton no less, his statue in Kelvingrove Park is the reminder of his contribution to Glasgow's story.

THOMAS LIPTON (1848–1931)

A child of the Gorbals, one of the world's greatest ever merchants remains a pin-up to entrepreneurial thinking and success. From the humblest of backgrounds – Lipton's Irish parents had left the Emerald Isle in desperate search of work after the 1845 Great Famine – he went to school at St Andrew's Parish but by his early teens was already seeking employment, helping his family out where he could. In 1868 he, like many Glaswegians of the time, sought to have his horizons broadened when he signed up as a cabin boy on a steamer that sailed from Glasgow to Belfast. Bitten by the bug and the prospects of the big wide world offered by imperial trading, he travelled to America to work on the tobacco plantations and to try his hand in new lines of endeavour, from sales to groceries.

He came home to Scotland in the 1870s and took his experience in the grocery trade to the streets of Glasgow, opening a store in Anderston. Clearly on to something, this soon became a chain as his reach spread across Britain. One of the early beneficiaries of clever advertising, his profits came quickly and he was said to be a millionaire by 30. However, his big breakthrough moment came with tea. Demand for the stuff was soaring and Lipton saw the opportunity to purchase tea gardens in the east and undercut existing tea sellers in Britain and America. By cutting out middlemen, his clever model allowed him to price tea at a level that was affordable to the working classes for the first time, thereby making it a drink for everyone and giving him free rein in an untapped market. He created Lipton Ltd in 1898, the same year he was knighted. You'll have doubtless bought a Lipton tea product at some point in your life and his legacy continues on shelves worldwide even now.

A lover of life, Lipton was a keen follower of sport, with a particular passion for yachting. Despite the astonishing wealth he accumulated, his legacy is also one of philanthropy. He contributed to the Red Cross during the First World War with the loan of his boats, and his compassion and support for the people of Serbia in particular led to an honorary citizenship of the city of Niš. Most tellingly though was the bequeathment of the majority of his estate upon his death to the people of Glasgow. It was the city that started him and made him and there is something very humbling in the fact that he felt the duty to give as much as he could back, presumably in the hope that others could follow, regardless of their starting point in life.

I sat beside him on a bench once in Sri Lanka, a bronze version of him anyway. On one of my more memorable

Thomas Lipton relaxing in Sri Lanka.

holidays, I was drifting around one day, not really paying attention as part of a self-guided hike to admire the plantations in what is a truly beautiful country, and was astonished to find a fellow Glasgow boy sitting there doing the same. With no one else around, I took pleasure in updating him on events from home, something I think he would have enjoyed.

WILLIAM BURRELL (1861–1958)

It feels slightly strange including someone on this very distinguished list for reasons not involving any particular skill or natural talent. Yet William Burrell's legacy to Glasgow and his contribution as a collector continue to keep his as one of the most recognisable names in the nation's cultural scene, and he deserves to be here for his generosity alone.

Born in Glasgow into a prosperous shipping family in 1861, his path to becoming a merchant was no great surprise. Taking over his father's business with his brother, they made significant profit from a savvy wheeler-dealer approach to ship purchasing and selling. Being a traveller, Burrell satisfied his love and passion for the arts by gathering in a remarkable and wide-ranging collection of pieces from all over the world. Over 9,000, in fact, and that included prints, paintings, tapestries, furniture and medieval stained glass. Known to be a man of refined taste and good judgement, he had an eye that his peers could only envy. It is said he bought his first painting aged just 15, trading it for his cricket bat. He collected fine Renaissance art from France including work by Manet, Cezanne and Degas, striking ceramics from China ... but also plenty of works from

Scottish artists that presumably were very dear to him as well. From what I've gathered about the man, he was one who had a deep desire to record times, places and experiences in his life and capture them in artwork. It was much more than just self-indulgence though, he very much wanted others to appreciate and enjoy what he did and he regularly donated to local galleries. He was also a Trustee of the National Galleries of Scotland and of the Tate Gallery in London. Burrell was knighted in 1927 for his services to art.

In addition to his vast army of pieces, he also left significant money to the city to be used for the construction of a suitable gallery where people could view his collection. It took some time to achieve this for him, but Pollock Country Park in the south of the city has, since 1983, held within its grounds his unique purpose-built memorial. The magnificent Burrell Collection remains one of the must-visits for locals and tourists, and reopened in 2022 after its latest comprehensive renovation. It provides a stunningly tasteful journey around one man's world – Glasgow has never had a more generous benefactor.

CHARLES RENNIE MACKINTOSH (1868–1928) AND MARGARET MACDONALD (1864–1933)

It was while studying at the inimitable Glasgow School of Art that a young Charles began his collaborative work on the art nouveau style. Encompassing textiles, furniture, watercolours, glass and metalwork, he would go on to become the most recognised architect and designer in Glasgow's story, and a household name to this day.

In 1897, through a contract won by his employers Honeyman and Keppie, his design for the new Art School was put into practice, with his most iconic achievement completed in 1909. From this early stage and throughout his career he had drawn on Eastern influences, with the delicate simplicity of Japanese styling clearly present in his works. To have studied at the school and then left it with a design that would inspire generations of students was the beginning of a remarkable journey that would continue long after his death. It was a hard blow to all Glaswegians when his masterpiece the School of Art was devastated by fire not once but twice in more recent times. Although the first blaze in 2014 could be redeemed with painstaking reconstruction, the unthinkable second blaze in 2018 reduced the building to its shell.

The art nouveau mark can be seen all over the city, with the recently restored Willow Tea Rooms being another favourite among his fans and students. Surely the most sophisticated place to enjoy tea and cake in the city, it was designed for Kate Cranston and opened in 1903. Within Glasgow University, a fabulous reconstruction of the Mackintosh House is open to guided tours and stunningly lays out the interior of the couple's immaculately stylish first home. Commissioned for work on and in private homes, commercial premises and public buildings, his was an astonishingly diverse portfolio, especially for what was a relatively short career. House for an Art Lover in Bellahouston Park in the South Side is another that draws in the crowds and is a particularly popular event and wedding venue. A personal favourite of mine is the Scotland Street School Museum in Tradeston just south of the Clyde. In imposing Baronial style and

The iconic Mackintosh at the Willow Tea Rooms.

decorated with eye-catching glasswork, the school is now a strangely evocative museum complete with authentically drafty corridors, echoing stairwells and stern classrooms. It would have been quite a place to begin an education, though it has not been in use as a school since 1979. Mackintosh and culture fans alike will love it.

Margaret was both an artist in her own right and wife and collaborator to Charles, the two going very much hand-in-hand in forming the Glasgow Style. The couple, along with Margaret's sister, Frances, and their friend Herbert MacNair, became known as 'The Four' thanks to their shared artistic preferences and identity. Together and separately they exhibited across Europe in the early twentieth century and their work is intertwined to showcase Margaret's floral style preferences to match Charles' rectilinear taste.

Curiously, their style was not particularly well received at home, and met with warmer interest internationally. They moved south to England in 1914 and then France in 1923. Passing on in 1928 from cancer, Charles would likely have had no inkling as to the extraordinary legacy he would leave. Another great artist underappreciated in his lifetime. Of course, the uncertain reception given among the Glasgow populace all changed after their passing, and Mackintosh remains among Britain's all-time favourite artists.

ALEX FERGUSON (1941–PRESENT DAY)

For many, he's the greatest football manager of all time. Overseeing staggering success as the boss of Manchester United from 1986 to 2013, this Glasgow boy has to be regarded as one of the biggest contributors to British sport.

Born in Govan, he was another to start life in a tenement. Playing football throughout his youth he, like so many city lads his age, combined his time on the pitch with work in the Govan shipyards. Showing enough promise to go full time in 1964 as a striker for Dunfermline, he returned to Glasgow by signing for Rangers for £65,000, which was a record fee at the time between Scottish clubs. Yet he never left Scotland as a player and failed to impress enough to make an impact at international level either, before his playing days ended in 1974.

Whatever his capabilities on the pitch, however, Ferguson's true calling was to orchestrate things from the sidelines. He was first appointed on a part-time basis as manager of East Stirlingshire, before quickly moving to Paisley-based St Mirren. In both roles, his no-nonsense, sometimes confrontational style have already been recorded by his former colleagues but victories on the pitch meant a big move to Aberdeen in 1978. He stayed in the north-east until 1986, recording some great successes, including upsetting the hierarchy by taking titles away from the two big Glasgow clubs and making an impact in European competition as well. Dons fans still reflect on the Ferguson years in wonder, and this earned him his career-defining move to the English giant Manchester United. Although not necessarily an immediate and consistent success, his tenure at United lasted right up to 2013 in an astonishing stint that was packed with silverware. Hundreds of his peers came and went from his rival clubs during his time in Manchester – victims of an increasingly sack-happy culture – but Ferguson could not be shifted. Dominant domestically for large periods of that time, Ferguson oversaw success at European level too, with United becoming European champions multiple times during his tenure. He built the kind of dynasty that still inspires awe.

The key to this success has been pondered by many over the years, with no one in football management able to emulate the Ferguson effect, and Manchester United slumping dramatically in the decade since his retirement. Certainly he had a level of control that other managers would envy; he ran the entire club in a very holistic way. He also gathered an enormous amount of respect from all in the game and it would be a brave opponent, journalist or player, who would cross him. Much of that respect was owed to his incredible record and longevity, but his personality and legendary combative nature were certainly factors, too. He had numerous well-documented fall-outs with players who stepped above their perceived station and his my-way-or-the-highway approach made for terrific entertainment among us football fans. An undoubted textbook disciplinarian and runner of a tight ship, he evidently loved a bargain on the transfer market, comparatively avoiding splurging the wasteful amounts being spent by competitor clubs from the turn of the century onwards, and ensuring Manchester United became one of the mightiest brands on the planet by tapping into new markets and fanbases. On the pitch, meanwhile, it was all about no flashiness, no showboating. Work hard, win big, go home. His teams were typically made up of hardy competitors, complemented by one or two individuals of astonishing flair and creativity. He was also a visionary, good at spotting and nurturing raw talent with countless young players exploding on to the scene, largely as a result of his good judgement, willingness to take risks and father-figure approach to educating.

Writing about the man's traits ... it's all so Scottish, so Glaswegian. It seems fair to say football may not see his like again.

BILLY CONNOLLY (1942–PRESENT DAY)

There's an exhausting number of modern-day actors, singers and creators that can count Glasgow as home. I'm thinking of the likes of James McAvoy, Robert Carlyle, Franz Ferdinand, Lulu and Scrooge McDuck. Old Scrooge aside though, none raise a smile quite as quickly as Billy Connolly. For so many of us he's the face and the heart of Glasgow, managing to capture the hardy cheek of the place through his acts and gigantic personality.

His journey to being maybe the greatest stand-up comedian, and very fine actor too, has been an extremely Glasgow affair. Born in Anderston during the Second World War, he was raised by his extended family in Partick and Drumchapel, with his father at war and his mother having left Connolly and his sister from a young age. He has talked about his challenging upbringing publicly, the abuse suffered at home and in school, and there's no doubt that he would not have been alone in such circumstances, when life in the city was desperately tough. Survive and get out seems to have been the mentality shared by many.

Starting his career in the shipyards (for his generation almost a prerequisite to a life in entertainment it seems), Connolly has talked of the banter on Clydeside with affection. Boys being boys to be sure, but there's something extra cutting about being on the receiving end of a merciless west of Scotland ribbing and his talent for comedy couldn't have had a better apprenticeship than dockyard Glasgow. Although a boilermaker by trade, there was obviously a creative flair to Billy that led him first to music, where he would gig his way around the folk pubs and clubs of Glasgow, and then into comedy. Audiences had no idea what was about to hit them.

One of his wonderful routines, the Crucifixion, told the story of the Last Supper, which has been tragically mis-portrayed

The Billy Connolly mural in the city centre.

as happening in the Holy Lands, because it really happened during a night out in Glasgow. Haven't you heard? Not Galilee, but Gallowgate. Controversial in his best couldn't-care-less way, the apostles are compared to drunken Glasgow pub-goers in a riot of foul language and tears-running-down-the-face hysterics. That was his way. Sensationally uncouth and infectiously friendly, you can find quick-witted characters of this type across Glasgow (alcohol tends to be involved) but Connolly's delivery was just sensational. A world-class specialist in toilet humour, swearing and self-deprecation, his style wasn't for everyone, but if you were a fan, chances are you were a huge fan. Connolly has also been a terrific actor over the years. Most memorably, he played Queen Victoria's devoted manservant in the 1997 film *Mrs Brown*. Forming a wonderful camaraderie with Judi Dench, he collected multiple BAFTA nominations for the moving portrayal.

Since announcing a diagnosis with Parkinson's disease in 2013, Connolly has been living a quieter life in the United States. Lucky them. Aside from the fact that I fear he may monopolise the conversation somewhat, he's definitely one I'd want at my fantasy celebrity dinner table.

NICOLA STURGEON (1970–PRESENT DAY)

Glasgow has long contributed greatly to the world of politics, by producing some of the greatest political minds. Former Prime Minister Gordon Brown was born in Giffnock, the first ever First Minister of Scotland, Donald Dewar, hailed from the city, too. Even the first ever Prime Minister of Canada,

John Macdonald, was a Glaswegian. But for the biggest political impact made on Glasgow and Scotland, the top spot has to go Nicola Sturgeon. Although originally from Ayrshire, she graduated from Glasgow University's Law School and her career began working for legal firms in the city. Since entering politics, her home and constituency as a Member of the Scottish Parliament was in Glasgow Southside (formerly Glasgow Govan).

With a career almost entirely dedicated to Scottish politics, Sturgeon joined the Scottish National Party in 1986 and rose steadily through the ranks, going on to have briefs in education, health and justice and to ultimately become leader of the party, and First Minister, in 2014. As Deputy First Minister at the time, she had championed the Yes Scotland campaign in favour of Scottish independence in the run-up to the 2014 referendum and was responsible for the legislative process behind it. Despite being on the losing side with a Scotland-wide vote share of 45 per cent (versus 55 per cent to remain tied to the United Kingdom), she was credited with hugely reinvigorating the constitutional conversation. Glasgow did, of course, vote yes to independence, also. Her popularity as First Minister throughout her tenure was remarkable given the politically divisive times at play during her term, with her communication skills emerging as her greatest strength. She sold out the Glasgow Hydro arena in record-breaking, popstar-esque time in 2014, when Scotland's political engagement level was sky high. And in elections at Scottish and British levels, her party completely dominated during her time as First Minister. Labour's own dominance of Scottish seats in Westminster ended, the SNP became the third largest party in the House of Commons (despite only being able to gather votes in Scotland) and the party membership surged to over 100,000. In addition to the furiously debated issue of independence, she led the nation through the COVID-19 pandemic and fallout from the United Kingdom's exit from the European Union. She was a brave and resilient captain of the ship during what was without question one of the most captivating and exhausting times to be a follower of Scottish politics.

Despite her clear successes, her time as First Minister closed in 2023 amid controversy over missing party donations, declining membership and no clear roadmap to achieving her party's central aim of independence. She was even very briefly arrested – though (at the time of this book's publication) not charged – as investigations into party finances began. Her sudden and surprising resignation left Scots to ponder her complex legacy. She was the first female to hold the top job in government, and the longest-serving First Minister too, at the time of writing. Her Cabinet choices promoted greater diversity than had ever been seen before and much had been done to raise the profile and equality within minority groups. Sturgeon even led the Glasgow Pride march in 2018 through the city centre. Many, however, would debate whether she advanced the push for independence enough, and many others would question her government's record in healthcare and education in particular. Few, though, would argue that she was one of the most talented and dedicated British politicians of her generation.

10

SPORT AND ENTERTAINMENT

As with Britain more widely, football is the undoubted leading sport of the city and Glasgow is home to the only two giants of the Scottish game, Celtic and Rangers. Ferocious rivals with huge worldwide fanbases, their mutual loathing has traditionally brought out the best and worst of us. Riveting on-field entertainment and countless edge-of-your-seat title battles have had to contend with the spectre of antisocial behaviour, sectarianism and reopening of historic Catholic–Protestant differences and intolerances.

Celtic were founded in 1887 and play their home games at Celtic Park in Calton in the East End. Their crowning moment came in 1967 when they defeated Internazionale in Lisbon to become the champions of Europe. Rangers came into being in 1872, playing at Ibrox in Govan, and have been historically the most successful club in Scotland domestically, with fifty-five league titles compared to Celtic's fifty-three, although Celtic have dominated the recent standings since 2011. On the continental stage, the inability of Scottish football to compete financially with the big leagues, particularly in England, has resulted in limited success for these two giants. Celtic's run to the UEFA Cup final in Seville in 2003 and Rangers reaching the equivalent in 2008 and in 2022 (the latter saw them only defeated on penalties by Eintracht Frankfurt) were notable exceptions, however.

European football has seen a handful of infamous stadium accidents in recent decades, and unfortunately Ibrox has witnessed more than one of them. As a 1971 game against Celtic was ending and the 80,000 fans were starting to file out, exiting before the final whistle to get home or to be at the front of the queue at the pub, a last-minute goal caused a burst of excitement in the stands at the previously problematic, and particularly steep, Stairway 13. A falling fan created a tumbling domino effect on the stairway that shockingly resulted in sixty-six deaths and hundreds of injuries in the crush, including children. These were before the times of all-seater stadiums, adequate toilets and painstaking safety procedures. The facilities at football matches were disgraceful, as fans' loyalties were taken for granted, and despite previous accidents and warning signs it took this loss to invoke overdue change, with safety made the top priority.

The Ibrox Disaster of 1971 was not even the first, with one of the same name dating back to 1902. This had been a Scotland versus England match and safety conditions were predictably even more basic. A completely uncontrollable horde of fans had gained access to the newly built stadium to watch the great rivals clash and the sheer weight of the mass crowd caused the collapse of a stand that plunged spectators into a pit of carnage.

Twenty-three died and over 500 were injured in what is thought to be football's first tragedy of this type.

The 'Old Firm' of Celtic and Rangers are not the only clubs in town, however, and Queen's Park and Partick Thistle have seen successes of their own, although not on a comparable level. The Jags, of Partick but playing in Maryhill, are my local team and these days tend to flirt between the top and second tier of the Scottish leagues. Although not blessed with anything remotely close to the trophy haul of the big two, they have a very loyal fanbase and an afternoon at Firhill is a great way for visiting football fans to enjoy a fairly friendly ninety minutes, if the furore of an Old Firm derby sounds a wee bit too intense. Queen's Park, meanwhile, were at the very vanguard of the game – founded in 1867, they are Scotland's oldest club and tenth oldest in the world! In my lifetime they've spent their time in the lower leagues, almost forgotten. But it was they who oversaw the formation of the Scottish Football Association and the first organised competitions across Scotland. They were my grandfather's team and my dad still checks their scores weekly in the hope of the long-sleeping giant making a return to the top table. It feels like it would be a great thing for football in Glasgow if they were to upset the duopoly.

Women's football has also grown impressively in recent years, with a surge in popularity helping in the breakaway from male-dominated fanbases. The 2022–23 season ended in the most thrilling of battles as Glasgow City pipped both Celtic and Rangers to the league title in the dying seconds of the final day.

Glasgow was host to the world's oldest international football competition in 1872, when Scotland and England battled out an anti-climactic goalless draw. The Scotland national team play their home games at Hampden Park in Mount Florida in the South Side, which also hosts the Scottish Football Museum.

MORE SPORT IN GLASGOW

Rugby has always gathered a passionate support across the British Isles, and Scotland games inspire plenty of good-spirited competitiveness, particularly in the Six Nations matches we play every year against England, Ireland, Wales, France and Italy. While it has traditionally lacked the game-of-the-people status enjoyed by football, the sport has followed a similar trajectory. In 1871 Scotland defeated England in the first international clash, while the following year saw Edinburgh District defeat Glasgow District in the first ever provincial match. Confirmation once again that everything started in Scotland, have I mentioned this yet? The Scottish Football Union – later the Scottish Rugby Union – was established in 1873, with Scotland playing their home matches at Murrayfield Stadium in Edinburgh going back to 1925.

The Glasgow Warriors, though, play their club matches at Scotstoun Stadium and compete in the annual European Rugby Champions Cup, the top-tier event for European club rugby. Starting as the amateur Glasgow District side in 1872, they became professional in 1996 and, following several rebrands, became the team of today in 2005. In the 2014–15 season they won the Pro 12, becoming the first Scottish team to win a major trophy. Although Scotstoun Stadium has a modest capacity of 7,351, the increasing interest in the team has led to calls to expand it to accommodate the ever-rising demand.

Cricket too has entertained a small segment of the population, pre-dating even the chasing of a football. The Partick-based West of Scotland Cricket Club was founded in 1862 and continues to welcome players to this day as a community amateur sports club. The Hamilton Crescent venue has hosted international contests including Scotland matches against the likes of Australia, New Zealand and the West Indies. Although the sport has never really taken off in Scotland – an oddity given its huge popularity in England – there are several other clubs still active in Glasgow, including one representing the university.

Although relatively small in scale, and much more reserved in the volume of its support, bowls has long been a player in the Glasgow entertainment scene. Greens are dotted around all over the city and it was one of the surprising standout events at the Commonwealth Games in 2014.

CINEMA CITY

The high streets of Glasgow today are a pale shadow of their predecessors, especially where nightlife is concerned. While there are some notable exceptions, fast food, neon lights and generic bars dominate. In the early twentieth century, streets would have been bustling with independent stores, locally sourced food and street performers creating a carnival atmosphere. Most loved of all in Glasgow were

the cinemas, with the Glaswegians of the day embracing
the American love of the movies and ensuring that picture
houses were ubiquitous. Going from short clips and side
attractions to the main event of an evening, films were
shown at the Theatre Royal and the Ice Skating Palace in
Sauchiehall Street.

By 1929, Glasgow had 127 cinemas – only our friends
over the pond could match that for commitment. They
had unapologetic architectural charisma and quickly
became central players in local communities across the
city's regions, whisking people off into places of fantasy
and dreams. Pringle's Picture Palace opened in 1907 and
was the first to have the exclusive purpose of showing
movies, which were starting to appear in colour around the
same time. The previous popularity of live performances
continued but were now being matched and exceeded by
this extraordinary concept of moving pictures. The Picture
House on Sauchiehall Street opened in 1910 and was the
best in all of Scotland. There was a fountain, caged birds
and palm trees to set the scene for this apparently exotic
experience. Renamed Gaumont in 1947, it lasted until
1972, with the likes of *The Sound of Music* among its best
screenings. La Scala, also established in a pre-pedestrianised
Sauchiehall Street, permitted one of the first TV dinner
experiences by allowing patrons to dine while watching.
Running from 1912 to 1984, it underwent a renovation
in favour of an increasingly popular art deco style in the
1930s, with a capacity up to 1,300. The Paragon Picture
House in the Gorbals was a converted former church. The
striking Odeon in Renfield Street would have turned plenty

of heads as competition raged. It was big enough to host live performances too, with the Beatles and the Rolling Stones contributing to its legacy. Closing in 2006, its white granite façade was looking deeply sorry for itself until 2019 but has been cleaned up and revived as a restaurant. The less-fortunate Lyceum, Govan's Super Cinema and another art deco gem, opened in 1938 but has been lying neglected, boarded up and empty since 2006. And the Granada Cinema on Duke Street in Parkhead has been demolished completely, one of many to sadly slip away.

Much credit must go to a man called George Green, one of the early entrepreneurs to seize on the craze. He created travelling booths that viewers could pile into to watch the short films of the day. Given the short lengths involved, the customer turnaround could easily be worked in his favour to turn a very tidy profit. His sons continued with this booming business after his death in 1915 and converted the Whitevale Theatre at Gallowgate and several other premises to build a mini empire of picture houses. The Green's Playhouse was their jewel in the crown, Europe's biggest cinema with 4,400 seats and even, in an eyebrow-raising design, a large dance floor on the upper level of the building. It ceased to be a cinema from the 1970s but still hosted some legendary live music performances from the likes of Elton John, Queen and The Who. Credit too to Walter Wilson, a retail businessman who started showing pictures in the late 1800s, initially for free. He opened a 500-seat theatre in his store and so successfully combined shopping and movies, a match made in heaven, and film was suddenly an affordable source of entertainment for the populace at large.

The Cinematograph Act of 1909 had ensured some minimal legal safety and licensing standards, and creators moved into niche genres including targeting children's entertainment needs. Popularity grew and grew, with movies becoming one of the few things that had more legs than any mere trend. So it continues today – the Cineworld on Renfrew Street was built on the site of Green's Playhouse, is the tallest in the world at 62m and has been the busiest in Britain, with 1.8 million admissions in 2003.

CENTRE STAGE

A place taken to the hearts of Glaswegians, particularly those in the West End, is the Kelvingrove Bandstand. Although a rare thing to spot these days, it was one of numerous examples of a bandstand to be found around the United Kingdom in the twentieth century, coming into being in 1924 and hosting rock concerts, military bands and international exhibitions. Up and coming Glasgow acts like Wet Wet Wet and Simple Minds were present during the boom decades for new music in Glasgow in the 1970s and '80s. Tragically forgotten during the 1990s, its lengthy restoration was completed in time for the 2014 Commonwealth Games. It has since hosted live performances from the likes of Tom Jones, Texas and Van Morrison, as well as comedy events and outdoor cinema screenings for those long summer nights. Laid out in an amphitheatre-like setting, it sits between Kelvingrove Park and Kelvingrove Museum and Art Gallery, with the River Kelvin running alongside. With a capacity of 2,500, it is an open and family-friendly space.

The view over the Kelvingrove Bandstand, beautifully set within Kelvingrove Park.

Modern-day festivals are some of the most anticipated in the Glasgow calendar, with the biggest of all being TRNSMT. Held every July in Glasgow Green, and starting in 2017, it spans three days but without the potential overnight camping chaos that contributed to the downfall of its predecessor, T in the Park. Over four stages, in the region of eighty acts perform to audiences of 50,000 music lovers per day. In its short history, the Scottish crowds have not disappointed, regardless of the weather. The Green also hosts the annual World Pipe Band Championships, where hundreds of bands from across the globe compete loudly and stirringly for their most prestigious honour. Watching these kilted performers putting their heart and soul into their music while being scrutinised by eagle-eyed judges is a tradition integral to Scottish heritage going back to 1947, and terrific fun to witness, even for complete novices.

Further festivals include the West End Festival and Glasgow International Jazz Festival. The former runs in June, going back to 1996, and has been referred to as 'Scotland's Mardi Gras'. There's live music, guided walks, street carnivals and ceilidhs, markets and more as the densely populated West End dances colourfully into summer. From riotously vibrant performances to sedate literary recitals, it's an event for all and 2023 saw WestFest deliver around 200 events across sixty venues. In the same month, jazz lovers traditionally flocked to the Merchant City in an event that has been high on the calendar since 1987. Now spanning around thirty venues dotted across town, gigs are performed over five days by Scottish and worldwide talents.

It was the mid-eighteenth century before theatres made an appearance, with initial resistance of the God-fearing variety flaring up to the extent that the first Playhouse on Alston Street was deliberately burned down. But this was not a tide that could be stemmed and the Theatre Royal was born in 1782, putting Glasgow on the entertainment map. It would be born again in Cowcaddens in 1869, where it still stands as the oldest theatre in town.

The Pavilion, opening its doors in 1904, embraced pantomime in the 1920s and '30s, meeting the demand for light-hearted distractions from the troubles of the time. The top artistes of the day brought their talents to its stage, including a young Charlie Chaplin. It remains much as it did then, on Renfield Street, and still presents family-friendly performances for audiences of the *Peter Pan, Aladdin* and *Treasure Island* variety. Of course, there's also still the Glasgow Royal Concert Hall at the top of Buchanan Street. It succeeded St Andrew's Halls after its destruction from fire in 1962 (and subsequent incorporating as part of the Mitchell Library façade) and opened in 1990. It is the primary venue for the outstanding Celtic Connections Festival that lifts all of our spirits every January.

The Citizens Theatre is the most grounded of them all, managing to tap into the pulse rate of everyday folks. It was established in 1943 by the screenwriter James Bridie and moved to its current site in the Gorbals in 1945, where its road has taken some twists and turns but never strayed too far from its core principles. The bosses got into hot water with the local authorities in the 1970s when they offered free entry to those possessing a trade union card, an act of solidarity between the performing actors and striking workers. Controversy continued with the use of nudity in several productions, with any associated outrage deafeningly drowned out by a frenetic clamour for tickets. The people had spoken. An army of British acting talent has worked at the Citizens and it has seen dozens of world premieres. Let's not forget The Tron, strikingly set on Trongate as part of one of the oldest buildings in Glasgow, a much-altered church with its origins in the fifteenth century. Fast forward to 1980 and it was bought by the Glasgow Theatre Club, which would go on to become the Tron Theatre Company, and that aimed to provide local creative talent with a platform. Stars including

Robbie Coltrane, Alan Cumming, Craig Ferguson and Peter Mullan have all been among them.

Finally, a special mention to the Phoenix Choir. Branching off from the internationally recognised Orpheus Choir that began in 1906 and disbanded in 1951, they lead the way in choral excellence in Scotland. They've recorded over thirty albums and can boast around 100 singing members who still perform across the UK, and occasionally in continental Europe. Their repertoire is extensive with performances at the Royal Albert Hall in London and Glasgow International Jazz Festival, showcasing a range of styles, from opera to pop. Youngsters have benefitted from their scholarship programme and they have strong connections with schools in Glasgow and surrounding areas.

YOU'RE HAVIN' A LAUGH

While Glasgow doesn't always make you smile, it will never fail you when in need of a laugh. We love to laugh. At the world, each other, ourselves ... and the comedy scene has thrived on this facet of the city's big personality. Of course, the comedians coming out of the city are legendary. Billy Connolly most of all but, more recently, Frankie Boyle, Kevin Bridges and the cast of *Still Game,* to name just a few. Boyle's dark cynicism tests limits daringly and hilariously, while Bridges is wonderful at nostalgic reflection on a Glasgow upbringing in the 1980s and '90s that resonates with my own millennial generation in particular. BBC Scotland's

Still Game is just a glowing tribute to how warm, grim, simple and somehow eternally inescapable our city can be for the ordinary pensioner. For all, though, Glasgow is interwoven in their performances and their material owes much to the home that we know, love and share. Tommy Morgan is one who many have forgotten but from the 1920s to the 1950s his was a particular brand of humour that the locals celebrated uproariously, at a time when tensions were high and audience expectations were demanding. God help the stand-up act that would fail to get the paying masses going. A specialist of the gallus cheek, Morgan was a regular at music halls and pantos across the city, with his timing and emphatic delivery setting him apart. Glasgow adored him.

These days, those in need can take in established and prospective acts at the Stand Comedy Club or the Glee Club, while the annual Glasgow International Comedy Festival has been attracting international big-name acts, alongside the best home-grown talent available, since 2002.

THE BARRAS

It seems almost criminal that it's taken me this long to dive into the institution that is the Barras, and its remarkable contribution to the city's tapestry. Everything is owed to the industriousness of Maggie McIver, whose vision endures long after her passing. The East End gathering spot in the Gallowgate is, in its most simple form, a market. A place for shopping, milling around, catching the gossip and snapping

The neon Barrowlands sign is one of the city's most recognisable symbols.

up a bargain. Yet it somehow – in a way that is hard to put a finger on – manages to be much more. A working-class hero to some, McIver became an unlikely business tycoon in a life epitomised by hard work and good sense. The daughter of an East End policeman and a French polisher, early life for a child of the 1880s was not one to inspire much encouragement. A happenstance opportunity to sell odds-and-ends goods from a barrow direct to market customers awoke a desire to upscale, which the teenager did rapidly. Her future husband, James, joined her in this street hawking venture as they sold local fruit and fish, first from hand carts, then from the multiple shops that they acquired. Locals and tourists still float around the market in droves at weekends, keen to grab a bargain among the most extensive range of produce that you could possibly imagine. Despite losing James in 1930, with nine children left behind, her relentless drive continued with the unearthing of a lucrative new venture.

Glaswegians' love for the dancin' has probably always been there but came to a head in the 1950s, when going for a boogie was all the rage among couples, friends or singles looking to put themselves in the shop window. Folk would pile on to the city's trams to start the partying early, hopefully with someone saying a prayer for the drivers. McIver's empire had expanded to include the famous Barrowland Ballroom, which started in 1934 and seized on this craze as a hugely popular dance hall. It was rebuilt in 1960 after a fire and its remarkable acoustics have seen it become a long-established concert venue.

THE TWENTY-FIRST CENTURY

GLASGOW IN THE MODERN ERA

In these opening decades of this new century, Glasgow embraced the new and saluted the old in its approach. Events and festivals became ever more prominent in the city calendar, and the population continued to swell in size and in its diversity. In 2007, the estimated population of the Greater Glasgow Urban Area exceeded 1.75 million citizens and a dynamic army of tourists, students and new residents have ensured a cultural vibrancy and energy to complement the air of tradition and weight of industries past.

Yet, the Clyde remains central to the city's soul. A shocking helicopter crash into the popular Clutha Bar on the riverbank in 2013 saw ten people lose their lives in an accident that struck very personally for all Glaswegians. Going back to the late 1800s, Cluthas were the passenger ships that nipped up and down the Clyde in its booming heyday, transporting for trade and tourism.

There's also, of course, the fantastic Riverside Museum that sits further along the Clyde and houses Glasgow's iconic transport arsenal. Everything from old trams and buses to sports cars and warships are among more than 300 items on display within the futuristic building. Designed in 2011 after a four-year construction project by Zaha Hadid, its style and vibe contrast superbly with the old-world Victorian charm of Kelvingrove's museum and make it among the most popular cultural attractions in the nation.

The prayers of impatient whisky lovers were answered with the opening of the Riverside's neighbour, the Clydeside Distillery, in 2017. Surely Scotland's most appreciated gift to the world, our whisky exports remain as central to our economy and identity as ever, with Glasgow now having a dram of her own to offer into the mix with the first centrally located distillery in the city in over 100 years. A comprehensive redevelopment of the traditional pump house delivered an

The Clutha Bar, now tinged with melancholy, has long been a favourite with locals.

impressive new hub for the water of life, with two stills and the capacity to deliver 500,000 litres per annum.

Just some of the offspring from the gigantic Clydeside regeneration work that has taken place in recent years, a partnership of enterprise bodies and governments have sunk millions into lifting the area out of the doldrums to create attractions and energy around the historic heart of Glasgow. Encompassing tourism, housing and commerce, recent years have seen an enormous effort to put the area back on the map with a corridor running for around 20km between the city centre and Dumbarton earmarked for investment. In addition to the Riverside Museum, the Hydro is one of the largest event venues in Britain, and on the south bank the Science Centre and Digital Media Quarter at Pacific Quay ensure a continuous bustle. The Clyde Arc – Squinty Bridge to locals – provides a stylish crossing of the river for vehicles and pedestrians, and housing blocks continue to pop up, too.

Life has returned to Clydeside, and to the city more widely through those globe-reaching tourism channels. Arguably going back to the hugely successful 1980s marketing campaign 'Glasgow's Miles Better' (than Edinburgh, of course), there has been a sustained rebranding effort to seize on Scotland's fabulous tourism potential and put the city on everyone's itinerary. The streets are vibrant again with the colourful murals, Mackintosh attractions still catch the eye of all who come, the museums and culture scene are as good as any in the United Kingdom, and shoppers, diners, sports and music fans of all styles and preferences are catered for as well.

Most nostalgic of all was the return of the paddle steamer *Waverley*. Having slipped away in the 1970s as a result of

The Saint Mungo mural by Smug, giving a modern twist to
'Glasgow's Father'.

dropping demand and increasing costs, she was sold to the Waverley Steam Navigation Company in 1973 for £1 in a move that allowed *Waverley* to continue her travels around Britain. A heritage rebuild was completed in 2003 with the result being a vessel closely resembling the famous original. Boiler trouble almost ended the illustrious story, save for a successful fundraiser of £2.3 million that returned her to the waters of the Firth of Clyde in 2020 for regular sailings. *Waverley* is the last seagoing paddle steamer in the world and makes for a memorable day trip to the holiday hotspots of the west coast for a new generation of Glaswegians heading 'doon the watter'.

Elsewhere, though, tragedy struck at the Glasgow School of Art, not once but twice, in the form of devastating fires that ravaged the iconic building and its exhibits. The first occurred in 2014, just when students were preparing to showcase their work, and was tackled heroically by firefighters, who somehow managed to preserve the vast majority of the building's integrity and contents. Estimates to restore the damage caused by the accident were noted at around £30 million. Although much painstakingly detailed planning was carried out, plans and spirits were crushed with an appalling second blaze in 2018 that finished off what the first did not. The damage was comprehensive, to the extent that the cause of the blaze could not be determined. At the time of writing there are plans to begin once more with a restoration, with the acceptance that even a best-case scenario would not deliver a completed school for many years.

Events have fuelled and sustained Glasgow in recent times, with the world's biggest artists and performers regular visitors, as we've seen in the previous chapter. The international sports scene has boomed, too. The 2002 Champions League Final was held at Hampden Park and saw Europe's most successful team, Real Madrid, collect yet another accolade for their cabinet under the Glasgow skies. As a nice bonus, the legendary French midfielder Zinedine Zidane volleyed home one of the most magnificent goals in football history to win the tie 2–1 against Bayer Leverkusen.

Most successful and memorable of all, however, was the coming of the Commonwealth Games in 2014 that saw another huge step taken to quash the stubborn negative image of Glasgow still held by many fixated on old and inaccurate assumptions. Seventy-one nations and territories were represented over eleven intense days in the summer heat, encompassing seventeen sports. More than 140 Commonwealth Games records were broken as gymnastics, athletics, aquatics, cycling and more grappled for spectators' attention. The spectacle was thrilling as Glasgow's impressive venues and immaculate facilities formed the foundation for something guaranteed to live long in the memory for all Glaswegians lucky enough to witness it. Those Glaswegians had plenty to be proud of too, as their welcome was warm, the atmospheres passionate and the behaviour impeccable.

Scotland had yet to see a festival on such a scale, with locals pouncing fast and around 1.3 million tickets sold. There were more women's and para-sports events than ever before. More than 12,000 local volunteers pitched in to keep the event running. Funding was poured into new walking and cycling paths, affordable housing was created within the Athletes' Village as part of an extensive Legacy Project and the city was unified and engrossed in a way I have certainly never experienced before. Accessible and inclusive, the feel-good factor was universal and no one would deny that a benchmark was set for all future Games to come.

Glasgow's history concludes with a look at the city of today. The city centre throbs with commercial activity and the retail scene is widely regarded as the best in Britain outside London. Yet the aftermath of COVID-19 and the economic squeeze of these challenging times has left too many streets looking neglected and unloved. Fortunately the plentiful green spaces, impressive and diverse dining culture and friendly buzz continue to make the quality of life potentially very high for those looking to settle. People for the Ethical Treatment of Animals awarded Glasgow the status of most vegan-friendly city in the UK in 2013, and 2023 sees Glasgow retain its two Michelin star restaurants in the form of Cail Bruich and

A view across the city centre including the Glasgow College building with its People Make Glasgow sign.

Unalome by Graeme Cheevers. But extremes linger. Inequality resides as noticeably as ever, with alcohol and drug-related problems rife and numerous areas seemingly left completely behind. In 2005, Glasgow's population life expectancy was 72.9 years, the lowest of any city in the UK, with shocking disparities between regions underlining the scale of the ongoing challenge for authorities. Improvements since then have been marginal, with Glasgow still dominating the spots at the bottom of the table. Those bleak realities aside, the energy emanating from the inexhaustible armies of academics mingle with the top-class music scene to give a modern culture and identity that makes the city tick, in the way that heavy industry used to.

And its people, the people of Glasgow that make it so, somehow carry all of that weight, old and new. They reveal it in their laughter and their cheek, their temper and their values. It's very hard not to have faith in them. Their honesty, grit and warmth are the first and last thing that come to mind – more than anywhere else I've encountered, its people *are* the city. May that never change.

ABOUT THE AUTHOR

Neil Robertson is a travel writer, blogger and presenter based in Glasgow. Writing exclusively about his home country of Scotland since 2012, he has travelled the length and breadth of the nation to unearth its stories and endless allure. Under the persona *Travels with a Kilt*, he has blogged extensively about the best of Scotland and has more recently moved into photography, videography and podcasting to reach new audiences. You can follow his adventures at travelswithakilt. com and across social media.

Having been born in Glasgow, he also studied and worked in the city before travelling and working internationally after graduating from Strathclyde University in 2009. He moved back to the West End in 2013, where he now lives with his daughter and his Golden Retriever, Harris. Neil also spends a large amount of his time in the West Highlands, where the mountains, lochs and coastlines provide him with the perfect playground for his outdoor passions.

BIBLIOGRAPHY

Antonine Wall, Bearsden, www.antoninewall.org

Bellamy, Martin and Spalding, Bill, *The Golden Years of the Anchor Line*, Stenlake Publishing, 2011.

Britannica, Scottish Enlightenment, www.britannica.com/event/ Scottish-Enlightenment

Brown, Alison, *Charles Rennie Mackintosh: Making the Glasgow Style*, Glasgow Museums, 2018.

Burrell Collection, blog, https://burrellcollection.com/the-burrell-blog-insights-from-the-project-team

Burrowes, John, *Great Glasgow Stories*, Mainstream Publishing, 2010

Charles Rennie Mackintosh Society, story, www.crmsociety.com/about-mackintosh/charles-rennie-mackintosh

Cinema Treasures, Glasgow Theatres, https://cinematreasures.org/ theaters/united-kingdom/scotland/glasgow

Connolly, Billy, blog, www.billyconnolly.com/blog/article/ billys-thoughts

Depardon, Raymond, *Glasgow*, Abrams, 2016.

Fry, Michael, *Glasgow: A History of the City*, Head of Zeus, 2017.

Gardiner, Robert, *The Golden Age of Shipping*, Book Sales, 2000.

Harris, Paul, *Glasgow at War*, Archive Publications, 1987.

Harris, Paul, *Glasgow Since 1900*, Flatman, 1988.

Historic Environment Scotland, Red Clydeside, https://blog. historicenvironment.scot/2019/01/red-clydeside-battle-george-square

History Scotland, Glasgow Trams, www.historyscotland.com/history/ the-glasgow-trams

History.com, Ibrox Stadium, www.history.com/this-day-in-history/ football-fans-crushed-in-stadium-stampede

History.com, World War I, www.history.com/topics/world-war-i/world-war-i-history

History.com, World War II, www.history.com/topics/world-war-ii/world-war-ii-history

Hunterian Museum, collections, www.gla.ac.uk/hunterian/collections/searchourcollections

Institution of Civil Engineers, Glasgow watersupply, www.ice.org.uk/what-is-civil-engineering/what-do-civil-engineers-do/glasgow-water-supply

Kingsley Long, H., *No Mean City*, Corgi, 1984.

Macfarlane, Colin, *The Real Gorbals Story*, Mainstream, 2007.

Meighan, Michael, *Glasgow: A History*, Amberley Publishing, 2015.

Mitchell Library, Thomas Lipton, www.mitchelllibrary.org/lipton/index.php

Moss, Michael and Hume, John, *Workshop of the British Empire*, Heinemann, 1977.

Murray, Bill, *Glasgow's Giants: 100 Years of the Old Firm*, Mainstream Publishing, 1988.

National Football Museum, Alex Ferguson, www.nationalfootballmuseum.com/halloffame/sir-alex-ferguson

Oakley, C.A., *The Second City*, Blackie.

Paddle steamer *Waverly*, history, https://waverleyexcursions.co.uk/welcome-aboard-waverley/history

Physics World, Lord Kelvin, https://physicsworld.com/a/in-praise-of-lord-kelvin

Reid, Jimmy, *Reflections of a Clyde-built Man*, Condor Publishing, 1976.

Stewart, Peter, *Glasgow West*, The History Press, 2005.

Stuart, Douglas, *Shuggie Bain*, Picador, 2021.

Terry, Stephen, *The Glasgow Almanac*, Neil Wilson Publishing, 2005.

The Alexander Thomson Society Story, www.alexanderthomsonsociety.org.uk

Twidale, Graham, *A Nostalgic Look at Glasgow Trams Since 1950*, Mortons Media Group, 1988.

Ward, Robin, *Exploring Glasgow – The Architectural Guide*, Birlinn, 2017.

Women's History Scotland, Suffrage Oak, https://womenshistoryscotland.org/2018/04/19/the-suffrage-oak-marking-100-years-of-women-living-and-growing-into-the-body-politic

INDEX